Presented by Ms. C.L. Marshall
July 20__

Critical Guides to French Texts

93 Mérimée: Colomba *and* Carmen

Critical Guides to French Texts

EDITED BY ROGER LITTLE, WOLFGANG VAN EMDEN,
DAVID WILLIAMS

MERIMEE

Colomba *and* Carmen

Peter Cogman

Senior Lecturer in French
University of Southampton

Grant & Cutler Ltd
1992

© Grant & Cutler Ltd 1992

ISBN 0 7293 0341 1

I.S.B.N. 84-599-3276-1
DEPÓSITO LEGAL: V. 748 - 1992

Printed in Spain by
Artes Gráficas Soler, S.A., Valencia
for
GRANT & CUTLER LTD
55-57 GREAT MARLBOROUGH STREET, LONDON, W1V 2AY

Contents

Preface

References to *Colomba* and *Carmen* in the text are to the two current Folio volumes of Mérimée's *Nouvelles complètes* with notes by Pierre Josserand: I, *Colomba et dix autres nouvelles*; II, *Carmen et treize autres nouvelles* (Paris: Gallimard, 1973 (1987 reprint) and 1974), as *Col.* and *Car.* respectively; these include, as well as all Mérimée's short fiction, the *Lettres adressées d'Espagne*. Italicized numbers in parentheses, followed by page references, refer to the numbered items in the select Bibliography at the end of this volume.

P.W.M.C.

1. 'Nouvelle', not Novel

Mérimée's career as a writer began, in the period between 1825 and 1830, with a flurry of works in various genres: drama, translated folk ballads, historical novel, short fiction. What is characteristic of them is that none sits happily inside a traditional genre. The playlets of his *Théâtre de Clara Gazul* (1825), purportedly translated from the Spanish by a fictitious Joseph Lestrange, subverted the neo-classical conventions of the French theatre, which were also under theoretical attack at the same time by Mérimée's friend Stendhal; so did the violent and unstageable historical drama *La Jacquerie* (1828). Both the Spanish plays and the Illyrian ballads of *La Guzla* (1827) were, though not published under his name, his own works, pastiches with elements of tongue-in-cheek exaggeration. His one historical novel, the *Chronique du règne de Charles IX* (1829), includes a notorious chapter (Chapter 8: 'Dialogue entre le lecteur et l'auteur'), in which Mérimée interrupts the narrative in order to refuse to give portraits of the 'grands personnages' of history, charged with their destiny, that the reader expects. In May 1829 he published in the *Revue de Paris* what is generally regarded as the first masterpiece of the French short story, *Mateo Falcone*, followed by a series of short works that in effect created a new genre in France.

No literary work emerges from a vacuum or simply from the 'genius' of an author. It is possible to point to various factors lying behind Mérimée's 'creation' of the *nouvelle* (*26*, p.4). These include literary models: there had been experiments in short narrative since the time of the French Revolution by Chateaubriand, Madame de Staël, Nodier, Benjamin Constant; 1828 saw the first translations into French, with enormous success, of the *contes fantastiques* of E.T.A. Hoffmann. The commercial difficulties of book publishing were another important factor: under the Restoration (1815-30) even

successful novels sold only 1,000 to 1,500 copies, and those largely
to *cabinets de lecture*; the effect of this was to keep book prices up
and production down, and to leave writers badly paid; literature took
refuge in journalism.[1] The final years of the Restoration saw a
sudden growth of the periodical press. This was prompted in part by
technical advances which had provided 'the essential tools for
manufacturing a mass literature as well as newspapers and periodicals in greater volume and for a lower price than ever' (*46*, p.55),
coinciding with a growth in the reading public, the result of the
spread of education and the growth of Paris and an urban middle-
class who preferred the immediacy of prose. Periodicals enjoyed
greater financial resources than the publishers of books (they were
subscribed to in advance, and so were able to adjust production to
sales and pay their contributors in cash). These circumstances all
contributed to the founding in 1829 of the *Revue des Deux Mondes*
and the *Revue de Paris*, which relied on short fiction as a basic
ingredient.

Dr Véron, founder of the *Revue de Paris*, published Stendhal,
Balzac, E.T.A. Hoffmann as well as Mérimée. His conscious attempt
to appeal to a diverse readership led him to impose certain stylistic
and thematic constraints on his writers: discretion in sexual matters,
not too many descriptions, digressions, or details, avoidance of
excessive length and excessive seriousness. He also imposed on
them specific requirements: to *entertain* above all, to 'attirer et
charmer' with 'œuvres rapides, d'un intérêt varié et accessibles à
tous'.[2] The frequently exotic subjects of these works avoid any
political dimension: the politics of the *Revue de Paris* was not to
mention politics. Recurrent themes and forms rapidly established
themselves, favoured by both writers and the public: the *conte
fantastique*, the story with a nautical setting (like *Tamango, La
Partie de tric-trac*), as reviews both created and responded to

---

[1] For the problems and the response of another writer at the same time, see
Roland Chollet, *Balzac journaliste: le tournant de 1830* (Paris: Klincksieck,
1983), pp.36-49.

[2] Dr Louis Véron, *Mémoires d'un bourgeois de Paris*, 6 vols (Paris: Gonet,
1853-55), III, pp.108-09, 103.

fashion. In this environment Mérimée seems to have found immediately an economic formula for the story which suited ideally both his particular talents and the requirements of the *Revue de Paris*.

In 1831 Mérimée became a civil servant, and in 1834, 'Inspecteur général des monuments historiques'. He wrote on archaeology and architecture, on history (Roman, Spanish, and Russian); he translated into French (from 1849) Pushkin, Gogol, and Turgueniev. In spite of the demands of his career and of these other activities, he continued intermittently to write and publish *nouvelles*, affecting to regard these 'petites drôleries' (*10*, IV, 374) as an amusement. These later stories are frequently longer, perhaps because he was no longer writing for the more formulaic requirements of the *Revue de Paris*, or Dr Véron's deadlines; they allowed Mérimée to develop both the thematic complexity of the stories and more elaborate, ironically structured frames for his narratives. Nevertheless, they are still recognizably not novels, unlike Constant's *Adolphe*, or Maupassant's *Pierre et Jean*, which are not dissimilar in length to *Colomba*. Nor can one usefully distinguish them from the earlier stories by using the two categories of *conte* for the shorter ones and *nouvelle* for the longer. These terms were used indiscriminately by Mérimée himself, who uses both terms about *La Vénus d'Ille* in one letter (*10*, V, p.200). A distinction between the two did gradually, and largely implicitly, emerge during the nineteenth century, as George has shown (*46*, p.9). It was based in part on formal considerations: on length (shorter *conte*, longer *nouvelle*) and on narrative technique (the *conte* being closer to an oral tradition and enjoying the impression of a story being told, leading up to a point which was often one that triggered the narration, whereas the *nouvelle* was structurally more complex). It was also based in part on thematic considerations that spring from length: the *conte* tended to focus on a single situation, while the series of incidents of the *nouvelle* allowed development of character or analysis of motive, or a preoccupation with the structure of the narrative itself. But this differentiation does not help with Mérimée's stories, which, whether short or long (and they range from half-a-dozen pages to over 150), partake of both categories.

A more useful distinction can perhaps be made by distin-
guishing his stories from the novel. This is one that Mérimée did
make, when he wrote, correcting himself significantly, about
Colomba: 'mon roman, ou plutôt ma nouvelle' (*10*, XVI, p.455). The
distinction cannot so much be made from the novel in absolute,
intrinsic terms, since it is a genre so hybrid that it can be almost
anything, but (as with most generic distinctions, which operate best
at a given time and in terms of the literary tradition and current
conventions) from the French novel of the nineteenth century, which
was the time when the novel too established itself as a major and
distinct literary genre.

All Mérimée's *nouvelles* were published in one instalment,
even the lengthy *Colomba*; they may have been abbreviated or
truncated, as was the case with *La Double Méprise*, but unlike many
nineteenth-century novels, they were never serialized,[3] just as he
seems to have read his stories aloud to his friends at one sitting.
(Here at least Mérimée echoes Poe's rather narrow prescription that a
short story should be read at one sitting, to 'avail itself of the
immense benefit of *totality*'.)[4] In all there is the characteristic
presence of a narrator's voice. This voice can be that of a character
involved in the events of the story either as the protagonist (the
lieutenant who narrates *Djoûmane*; don José in *Carmen*) or as a
witness to events, sometimes completely fictional (Wittembach in
Lokis), at others to some extent resembling Mérimée but distinct
from him (the Narrators, as I shall call them, of *La Vénus d'Ille* and
Carmen, both archaeologist-historians on field trips). Alternatively
the voice can be that of a narrator who does not belong in the world
of fictional events, as in *Mateo Falcone* or *Colomba*, but one who
always in Mérimée clearly signals his presence ('je') to the reader.
The narrator's voice plays an important role in the novels of Balzac

---

[3]Mérimée criticized the *roman-feuilleton* where, he said, the reader has often
forgotten yesterday's chapter and consequently only half understands today's
(see *12* , p.119).

[4] 'Twice-told Tales', Edgar Allan Poe, *Selected Writings*, Harmondsworth:
Penguin, 1967, p.446.

and Stendhal, but it is one which Flaubert and Zola sought to eliminate.

Whereas the nineteenth-century novel, most explicitly in Balzac and Zola, sought to explain man, the *nouvelle*, with less space available, is less interested in causes than in effect; as Paul Bourget argued, 'elle pose le fait, brut et détaché' (*20*, p.19). On the one hand this tends to mean (in terms of form) works characterized by density, convergence, concentration on one significant moment or decisive episode, rather than ones that diverge, expand, develop into a series of episodes (*20*, p.12); the novelist seeking to create an illusion of totality, breadth, continuity, whereas the *nouvelle* privileges the isolated moment or episode and a very structured narrative controlled by a narrator. This can lead to a narrative that is much more obviously patterned than is generally the case in the novel. But brevity and the interest in effects rather than causes can also have consequences as regards characterization and theme. It can lead to simplification of character and lack of development, a closed image of man corresponding to a closed form. It can produce emphasis on a certain sort of character, isolated, marginal, or at odds with social norms (*49*, p.27), like don José, as opposed to the individual finding his way inside society who is characteristic of the French novel of the time (Rastignac, Julien Sorel). It can lead to concentration on effects of shock and surprise, with intense, violent, cruel, or perverse passions. The limitation of the forces involved tends to lead to sharply contrasted pairs (law versus freedom; the primitive versus civilization), and intensify the opposition, the conflict and the resultant violence. Much of the nineteenth-century novel tries to portray the typical, the ordinary, the everyday; the short stories of Gautier, Mérimée, Barbey d'Aurevilly, Villiers, and often Maupassant, although they present their events and characters as (at least initially) belonging to the 'real world', like those of the novel, are frequently the domain of the supernatural, the exotic, the bizarre, the strange and the shocking, lending force to Goethe's view of the subject of a *Novelle* as 'an unheard-of event that has occurred'.[5]

---

[5]'Eine sich ereignete unerhörte Begebenheit' (*Gespräche mit Eckermann*, 29 January 1827).

Such generalizations should remind us that content (characters, themes, events) and technique are interdependent; and that short fiction is not something *less* than the novel, except in terms of length, but something whose different formal constraints produce different sources of interest and pleasure. But generalizations are only useful as a starting-point, to be tested against the more complex reality of individual stories. I shall discuss *Colomba* and *Carmen*, two major works of Mérimée's maturity, in parallel. They raise common issues: the use of borrowed material, of exotic settings and local colour, the respective values of the primitive and the civilized. In their portrayal of a Corsican girl drawing her brother, a French officer, into a local vendetta, and a gypsy girl leading a Basque soldier into a life of smuggling, robbery, and violence, both present similarly strong-willed heroines set against men torn between conflicting allegiances. The tales contrast in their narrative technique: *Colomba* is told by a narrator external to the characters and events, *Carmen* by an archaeologist who meets, in a frame-narrative, the protagonists, one of whom subsequently tells him his tale; I shall try to show both the different effects Mérimée can draw from these different techniques and the points they share.

2. Imitation and Irony

From the nineteenth century, Mérimée has frequently been characterized as lacking in imagination. 'Je soupçonne qu'il n'a jamais fait une œuvre d'imagination pure; je crois qu'il a peu créé. Le don de la vie semble lui avoir été refusé', wrote Louis Enault in 1853 (quoted in *1*, III, p.253), and the judgement has been frequently echoed. A large part of his fictional output relies to a great extent on *pre-existing* material. His preface described his historical novel *Chronique du règne de Charles IX* as 'un extrait de mes lectures'; some of his *nouvelles* are reworkings of previous tales: in the case of *La Vénus d'Ille* there are so many 'sources' that it is difficult to know which was (or were) Mérimée's starting-point. His first short story, *Mateo Falcone*, written before he had visited Corsica, is a reworking of a standard Corsican tale of a shepherd executed by his family for betraying two deserters (or in some versions, one) for money. It exists in several versions, and had just been retold in July 1828 in an anonymous article in the *Revue trimestrielle*. The vendetta that was the basis for *Colomba* had been evoked in the *Voyages en Corse, dans l'île d'Elbe et en Sardaigne* published in 1837 under the pseudonym Valéry, which recorded the recent (1833) vendetta in the village of Fozzano (near Sartène, in the south of the island) between on the one hand the Durazzo and Paoli families, and on the other the Carabelli and Bartoli families, a feud which had led to several deaths and an ambush in which the son of Colomba Bartoli (née Carabelli), the moving spirit in her clan, had been killed. It had been concluded by a peace treaty in 1834, but the hatred of Colomba Bartoli remained fierce and her reputation, indeed legend (*32*, p.183), spread through Corsica. After Valéry's evocation of this figure, 'âgée de soixante ans, mais verte encore' who 'malgré la douceur de son nom, fut jadis une véritable amazone, et tirait fort joliment des coups de fusil' (quoted in *32*, p.112), she almost became a local curiosity, and travellers called to hear her tell her story. Mérimée himself visited her on his tour of Corsica to survey the monuments in 1839 and no doubt heard the story of the vendetta from her and others on the island ('Je ne me lasse pas de me faire conter des histoires de vendettes', *10*, II, p.288). The figure of Jérôme Roccaserra, author of the *coup double*, who (on his account, at least) killed two enemies in a chance meeting (*30*, pp.460-63), although wounded in the arm, was likewise already well known. The same combination of pre-existing stories that he had been told or read about, and personal material acquired in the course of his travels, lies behind *Carmen*, which draws on the encounters and anecdotes described in Mérimée's own *Lettres d'Espagne*, and a real event that (according to a letter to her) the comtesse de Montijo had told him in 1830:

> Il s'agissait d'un Jaque [brave, fanfaron] de Malaga qui avait tué sa maîtresse, laquelle se consacrait exclusive-ment au public. ...Comme j'étudie les bohémiens depuis quelque temps avec beaucoup de soin, j'ai fait mon héroïne bohémienne. (*10*, IV, p.294)

This both makes his oral source clear, and shows that Mérimée from the start feels free to adapt the basic datum of both main characters' origins (basic in that the story hinges on the difference of cultures between Carmen and don José). In much the same way he makes his Colomba a young girl, whereas the real Colomba Bartoli was 58 in 1833, an embittered mother who had lost her son in the feud, and transfers to her the youth and beauty of her daughter whom he had met in 1840 (the only account we have of this is in a letter by Mérimée (*10*, II, p.289) that does not seem free of fictional trans-position either: it is quoted in *Col.*, p.504).[6]

---

[6] The daughter was in fact 31, not 20, at the time, and had a lover whom she was to marry in 1843.

The extent and nature of these changes to his sources is, however, not always clear. In both cases problems have been posed for later critics by the seemingly irresistible urge to fill in the gaps of our ignorance and rewrite the facts, especially when they are uncertain, using Mérimée's fiction, and by the willingness of the descendants of participants, or at least the family of Colomba Bartoli, to remodel their past on Mérimée's story. In the case of *Carmen*, assisted by our ignorance of what Mme de Montijo actually told Mérimée and whom he met in Spain in 1830, critics have dreamed up a 'real' Carmen: if he records in a *Lettre d'Espagne* meeting 'une très jolie fille, point trop basanée' (*Car.*, p.419) called Carmencita, suspected by his guide of being the daughter of a *sorcière*, and sketches her, this becomes the 'première rencontre avec une Carmen dont Mérimée s'est souvenu en 1845' (*6*, I, p.396). In fact Mérimée does not say that the girl was a gypsy; Carmen's complexion is dark; she initially strikes the Narrator as 'une femme' (*Car.*, p.108). In the same way the bandit José Maria evoked in another *Lettre d'Espagne* has been made a model for don José, to the extent of talking of 'la rencontre de Mérimée et de José Maria' in the first chapter of *Carmen* (*1*, III, p.212; *19*, p.211). Mérimée's point seems however to be to suggest differences between the two figures. José Maria is 'beau, brave, courtois' to victims, flatters women ('Les Voleurs', *Car.*, p.405), has a 'physionomie ouverte et riante' (*Car.*, p.406). It was the attempted seduction of a 'demoiselle de bonne famille' that led to violence and his flight, after which he turned to smuggling for money. He is not the don José of *Carmen*, but rather the 'generous bandit' of Romantic myth, showing 'les vertus chevaleresques des anciens preux' (*Car.*, p.412), munificent like Robin Hood (to whom he is explicitly compared, *Car.*, p.405). The only real parallels between the two figures are that both were destined for the Church (*Car.*, p.406) and that both have links with gypsy girls (*Car.*, p.411).

This suggests the complexity of Mérimée's relationship with his sources. The main stories are provided from sources, both literary and oral; for local colour (see Chapter 3 below) Mérimée draws on his wide reading and observations at first hand from his travels. But they are altered in key respects, so that if José Maria still figures in *Carmen*, it is as someone very different from the protagonist don José, — as a shadowy double who is simultaneously the mythical Romantic bandit of the *Lettre d'Espagne* and of travellers' tales, whom the Narrator yearns to meet, and a real figure known and treated with some condescension by don José, who seems (from the hints he drops) the better bandit and a lover who manages to keep *his* women by being unfaithful to them and ill-treating them.

Moreover both tales have, as has been often noted (first of all by Mérimée's contemporary, the critic Sainte-Beuve),[7] a literary model as well. In the case of *Colomba*, this is the Greek tragedy of Electra, notably in the version by Sophocles. Electra's father Agamemnon had been murdered (on his return from the Trojan war) by her mother and her lover Aegisthus; Electra kept her desire for revenge alive, awaiting her brother's return. Orestes returns from abroad, and encouraged and helped by his sister, carriers out the act. Both works share a fierce and virginal heroine, and a basic situation where they are calling on their brother to avenge the murder of a father; it is possible to see more specific echoes between situations (there are moments when both heroines think that their brother is dead) and even language, in the use of bird imagery in Colomba's *ballatas* and by Electra (the nightingale mourning Itys, ll.147-49) in Sophocles' tragedy. But there are also crucial differences: Colomba's desire for vengeance springs solely from her sense of the family, Electra's and Orestes', from filial piety but also from the Gods (Apollo's oracle); Orestes returns with the deliberate aim of carrying out vengeance; Colomba's is carried out on someone outside the family, and the potentially tragic consequences of Orso's action are evaded; Orestes has to murder his own mother as well as Aegisthus. The role of the chorus in Sophocles is frequently to calm down Electra, whereas the villagers are spurring Orso to act.

In the case of *Carmen*, the model is the eighteenth-century novel *Manon Lescaut*, whose heroine leads the young noble des Grieux astray into a life of card-sharping, theft, and murder. The

---

[7] For *Colomba*, see *33*, pp.490-92; for *Carmen*, see 'Les Faux Démétrius', *Causeries du Lundi* (Paris: Garnier, s.d.), VII, pp.371-88.

woman in both cases is the strong or active personality, dominating events; they lead to the degradation of two 'decent' men who become attached to them; they are seen by the men, who are jealous and possessive, as fickle, and exploit their own sexual attraction (as women of a lower social class than the hero, and apparently thereby possessing a more immediate sexuality) with 'various degrees of illegality' (*39*, p.60); they lead their lovers into scenes where they dupe and exploit foolish rich men; in both cases events lead to the death of the woman (Manon dies of exhaustion in America, in a last flight with des Grieux from the law), and both lovers bury their mistress in graves they have dug with their own weapons (sword or dagger). There are also numerous structural similarities between the stories: both lovers tell their tale to a frame-narrator, who helped them when met on a previous occasion (thus setting up a debt which motivates the telling of their tales); in both cases this first meeting is late on in the relationship with the woman; the women, Manon and Carmen, though seen largely through the eyes of their lovers, are also seen by the frame-narrators who, as trustworthy observers, serve as independent witnesses to their charm.

In both cases, however, it is not so much a question of 'sources' as Mérimée writing a story with obvious echoes of a pre-existing literary work, whether he was fully aware of it or not, and one in both cases with archetypal resonances. Nor do the parallels mean that there are not also crucial differences (unlike Manon, Carmen never claims fidelity in love to don José). We are aware of parallels that enrich our reading of both stories. Behind the local colour of *Colomba* lies a basic and primitive pattern of vengeance that is not just a specific product in Corsica of historical circumstances (the period of Genoan domination of the island having created a lack of faith in the judicial system and a recourse to private justice), but something that stretches back to antiquity; behind the exotic setting and colourful characters of *Carmen*, we sense the destructive force of relationships across cultural and social barriers, the pattern of a weak man relating to another man his fatal involvement with a woman who (in his eyes) is ultimately to blame.

As Cellier has pointed out, 'le dénouement de *Carmen* suggère la solution radicale pour mettre hors d'état de nuire la *donna mobile*. Des Grieux, comme don José, devait supprimer Manon' (*34*, p.263). *Carmen* takes *Manon Lescaut* one stage further by making the hero physically murder the heroine, thus showing that the underlying force of the story is not just for the man to blame the woman for his wasted or criminal life, but to kill her (the same pattern can be seen in Constant's *Adolphe*, another confessional narrative about a fatal love-affair where the hero wastes his life and indirectly brings about the death of the heroine). In other words not only are the other stories echoed in *Carmen*, but *Carmen* points to a possible way of reading other stories which have the same underlying pattern, by pushing certain aspects to their logical conclusion; and it is only *one* possible way: other aspects of the story of Manon also feed into the Romantic theme of the prostitute in love, redeemed by love (*34*, pp. 267-68).

Irony

Yet at the same time all Mérimée's stories bear a strong personal stamp. To specify this it will help to consider briefly the general tone of his narrative, before moving on to consider what he presents. The personal stamp is due not just to the themes that attract him: passion, violence, the association between sexuality (particularly wedding-nights) and death, the exotic. It springs as much from the way they are treated, for which a convenient general term could be irony. In the most everyday sense a word or statement is ironic if it is the opposite of what the speaker really means: the narrator refers to Lydia's decision to stay in Corsica and kill time painting as 'cette *généreuse* résolution' (*Col.*, p.335) when it is clearly seen as a product of her vanity and desire to preserve an image as an intrepid traveller in her eyes and in the eyes of others. The archaeologist of *Carmen* refers to his 'minces connaissances' (*Car.*, p.173), expecting us to understand 'considerable'. The irony arises from our sense of a discrepancy (here, between what is said and what is meant), not explicitly pointed out, which establishes a sense of collusion between narrator and reader. Insofar as it relies on the intelligence of the audience, it shows Mérimée consciously aiming at a sophisticated, intelligent public. At the same time it often seems to play with and so call into question the set (moral) attitudes of society generally: playing with its 'received' language.

The sense of ironic discrepancy can equally come from a gap between a character's expectations, or ideas, and reality (Lydia sees Orso's 'vastes desseins' (*Col.*, p.332), whereas we know that he has returned to Corsica to sell property and marry his sister off (*Col.*, p.357)). But it also lies behind Mérimée's use of local colour euphemisms for violence which seem strange or inappropriate to the reader: Castriconi calling the bandits' guns 'passeports' (*Col.*, p.391); Brandolaccio referring to the Barricini sons as Orso's 'gibier' (*Col.*, p.436) (echoed involuntarily later by Nevil when he tries to reassure Colomba by saying that the shots she heard were Orso 'hunting': *Col.*, p.442). This incongruity, by appearing to balance and so give equal weight to the pedantry of the archaeologist-narrator of *Carmen* and to passion, to Lydia's vanity and to matters of life and death, seems a denial of the serious (*12*, p.182). The account of the funeral of Mme della Rebbia is presented in a veil of legal and formal language (the mayor, a lawyer, is involved): 'Le jour de l'enterrement, les deux partis se trouvèrent en présence, et l'on put craindre un moment qu'un combat ne s'engageât pour la possession des restes de Mme della Rebbia' (*Col.*, p.352); the language is at odds both with the violent feelings of those involved (the colonel is 'furieux') and the macabre comedy of the battle over the mortal remains of Mme della Rebbia. The comedy implies a detachment from the issues that so grip the characters; the reader can see highlighted the paradoxical results and bizarre aspects, in a way that they cannot. The feud produces a water supply for the village as a result of clan rivalry (*Col.*, p.374).

Incongruity can also take the form of inappropriate cultural references. At a point of high tension in *Colomba* (the mutilation of Orso's horse), Mérimée inserts a parodic reference to the fable-writer La Fontaine (*Col.*, p.427) and indicates it by inverted commas. This distancing is all the more notable in that Mérimée's aim is a style that is neat, elegant, and fresh, but almost totally inconspicuous; one that refuses lyricism, eloquence, and any attempt to call attention to itself. By the simple structure of short sentences, and the avoidance of subordinate clauses, Mérimée creates a 'calm and measured' style, the impression of being 'undisturbed by the vicissitudes of life' (*12*, p.193).

Characteristically in Mérimée, a sense of distance can be created by the clear and rapid narrative of disconcerting or bizarre events, presented as quite natural, or the unemotional narration of violent or shocking events, related dispassionately and with attention not to the emotion of the character involved but the precise physical way things happen. This is particularly the case with violent deaths: the revolt of the slaves in *Tamango* (*Col.*, pp.67-68), or the way Saint-Clair falls when fatally wounded in the duel in *Le Vase étrusque*. Thus with the account of the fight with Garcia given by don José.

> Garcia était déjà ployé en deux comme un chat prêt à s'élancer contre une souris. Il tenait son chapeau de la main gauche, pour parer, son couteau en avant. C'est leur garde andalouse. Moi, je me mis à la navarraise, droit en face de lui, le bras gauche levé, la jambe gauche en avant, le couteau le long de la cuisse droite. Je me sentais plus fort qu'un géant. Il se lança sur moi comme un trait; je tournai sur le pied gauche et il ne trouva plus rien devant lui; mais je l'atteignis à la gorge, et le couteau entra si avant, que ma main était sous son menton. Je retournai la lame si fort qu'elle se cassa. C'était fini. La lame sortit de la plaie lancée par un bouillon de sang gros comme le bras. Il tomba sur le nez, raide comme un pieu. (*Car.*, pp.154-55).

One brief mention is made of don José's feelings. The focus of attention is not on the individuals as a whole, but on parts of the body (throat, chin, nose) and of weapons (the blade). Mérimée notes odd effects (the blood expelling don José's broken blade); humans lose their individuality: Garcia is initially a cat, and at the end falls like a post. What we like to think of as crucial moments of life and death pass with shocking rapidity ('C'était fini'). The narrative is not quite what we (conventionally) expect as appropriate (which would include emotional tension, a struggle with reversals of fortune perhaps); the incongruity serves to call into question what is (what we accept as) 'normal', to startle us with an abrupt confrontation with something that strikes us as 'real'.

Characteristic of Mérimée's tales is the reader's frequent sense of the inappropriateness of a witness or narrator to the events witnessed or related. Like the Narrator of *Carmen*, those of *La Vénus d'Ille* and *Lokis* are academics (in the case of *Lokis*, a pastor who has postponed his marriage for linguistic research) dealing with events of passion and violent death. The archaeologist's frame-narrative in *Carmen* serves to introduce this inappropriateness (though it does have, as we shall see, thematic links with the tale of don José); even when don José's narrative is under way, he is present in the footnotes; in the final chapter he reappears to displace entirely any interest in don José and Carmen with an ethnographic and linguistic account of gypsies. This chapter[8] carries to an extreme the idea of an incongruous witness or inappropriate narrator by showing one who has seemingly lost all interest in the characters and their passions. The Nevils are the least likely witnesses to a vendetta. The colonel is preoccupied solely with hunting and food, even at dramatic moments (when the news comes of the crucial ambush), and remote from

---

[8] It was added in the 1847 publication of the story: it did not appear in the original version published in the *Revue des Deux Mondes* in 1845. It has puzzled or irritated many commentators. Some have dismissed it as an irrelevant appendage which has nothing to do with the rest of the work (*14*, p.61); others have justified it in terms of (more or less plausible) motives derived from Mérimée's psychology, social position, or career (a triumph of the antiquarian Mérimée over the writer of fiction (Filon, *15*, p.73), an attempt by a respectable civil servant, historian and Academician to excuse writing a spicy tale (*37*, p.118)). For other critics the exaggerated erudition of the final chapter is linked to the start and attempts to achieve an effect on the way that we react to don José's narrative, prompting us to dissociate ourselves from the archaeologist-narrator and identify or sympathize with don José (*12*, p.170).

Corsican reality in all other respects, ingenuously referring to the coroner and the country house of M. Brandolaccio. Lydia may be fascinated with the *sauvage* and the *primitif* that have attracted her to Corsica, but her expectations are Romantic and conventional and she is shocked by the reality of events, the *maquis* and the bandits; her sentimental flirtation with Orso and weak feelings are set against Colomba's strong passions.

What is the effect of this presentation on the reader? Does it, and do Mérimée's ironic strategies generally, intensify the emotion and passion, restrain them and so reinforce them (*6*, II, p.341)? Or do they mute their effect by distancing them, creating a distance between events and reader and decreasing the force of the tale (*12*, p.171)? It would seem that they have to do one or the other, and that it is straining the argument to see them doing both at the same time (*1*, III, pp.xxxi-ii). What the irony, the incongruous narrator or witness, does is perhaps not so much to *intensify* the emotion and passion as to enable the reader to see it and its ambiguous effects much more sharply, while holding it at a distance as something both fascinating and dangerous. It brings it into sharp focus, but that clarity is a function of a certain non-involvement. In this way it reflects the ambiguity which, as we shall see, characterizes Mérimée's fascination with the primitive. Mérimée's concern, all the time, as a writer, especially of short fiction, is with form, structure, control. His view of man and life lead him to stress uncontrollable passions, misunderstandings, self-deception, chance, and fate. The resultant fiction is a 'combination of highly controlled narrative craft and uncontrollable feeling' (*17*, pp.130-31), in which the ironic tensions set up by inappropriate words, witnesses and narrators are a key element in its fascination.

3. The Exotic

Spain, Corsica: these (like the settings of many of Mérimée's *nouvelles*) are, for the nineteenth-century French reader, exotic. The exotic fascinated the early nineteenth century, which had come in contact with it for various reasons: politically, the emigration had taken the French abroad, as had the wars of the Revolution and the Empire; intellectually, English, Spanish, German and Italian literature was being discovered in translation under the Restoration; materially, Waterloo and the peace it brought in Europe had led to more travel, as did the improvement in roads, the introduction of steamboat services, eventually of railways: the word *touriste* entered the French language in 1816 and it is italicized at the start of *Colomba* as a neologism. The taste for the exotic was reinforced by a desire to escape a present felt as increasingly mediocre, unexciting and materialistic: what the critic Sainte-Beuve called 'notre époque blasée et nivelée' (*25*, p.198). Spain had played a role in recent French history both in the guerrilla war against Napoleon's invasion and in the intervention of French troops in 1823, but it was little known at first hand and difficult of access. Corsica was French territory, but only since 1768 when Genoa had ceded the rights to France, and had only been integrated into France since 1789. Not only the countries, but the class of the characters (the brigand and gypsies of *Carmen*, the bandits of *Colomba*) could offer the cultivated French reader what Mérimée said about the charm of picaresque novels: 'un voyage dans un monde inconnu' (*2*, IX, p.19).

The discovery of the exotic went hand in hand with an intellectual awareness of the differences between societies both externally (costumes, customs) and morally (behaviour, attitudes, values) that could be summed up under the key Romantic phrase 'couleur locale'. The eighteenth century had grown to appreciate both external local colour and its picturesque possibilities, and the differences between other (Indian, Oriental) societies and the Christian West, often using the difference to satirize accepted European social, political or religious attitudes. Victor Hugo's Romantic manifesto, the *Préface de Cromwell*, had stressed the importance of local colour; but that of many literary works around 1830 (e.g. Hugo's *Les Orientales*, Musset's *Contes d'Espagne et d'Italie*) owed more to reading than first-hand knowledge, and even more to their authors' excited imaginations, and frequently took the form of the superficial use of local terms whose main effect is unintelligibility.

From his early work Mérimée had been fascinated both with the 'local', that which was characteristic of a time and place, in his portrayal of behaviour, and with 'colour', not just with the purely external and picturesque, but with any signs of energy, violence and passion in different, more 'primitive', societies. At the same time this side of his temperament, which one could term Romantic, was counterbalanced by a cool and sceptical detachment which held him back from any positive commitment, a critical intelligence, a distrustful lucidity. Before 1830 his evocation of the exotic was based on books, and in the case of his Spanish theatre and Illyrian ballads, had an element of spoof: he knew that an illusion of authenticity can be faked. *Le Vase étrusque* mocks infatuation with a local colour based on the use of exotic terms (*Col.*, pp.89-90). What we find in both *Colomba* and *Carmen* is an abundance of local colour (in both senses: the characteristically local and the picturesquely vivid), both as regards local customs and attitudes and local language, based on wide reading and also on first-hand experience of both countries, but one aimed essentially at highlighting human behaviour. 'C'est la pure nature qui m'a plu surtout', he wrote to a friend from Corsica: 'Je ne parle pas des vallées, ni des montagnes, ...mais je parle de la pure nature de l'HOMME. Ce mammifère est vraiment fort curieux ici...' (*10*, II, p.288). (The use of 'curieux' typically betrays an interest in events as *different* and a certain aloof detachment.) At the same time he maintains a distance from the slogan of local colour, constantly treated ironically (*Col.*, p.315: 'Explique qui pourra le sens de ces mots'), and from the attitude of dilettante curiosity fuelled by a literary imagination represented by Lydia (and to some extent the Narrator at the start of *Carmen*). This irony towards the term was not peculiar to Mérimée. Théophile Gautier described in his *Voyage en Espagne* (evoking a trip in 1840, and first published in 1843)[9] a soup coloured with saffron as offering 'de la couleur locale, de la soupe rouge!' (p.50): it was a term debased by ten years of overuse, that could no longer be taken seriously.

How then does Mérimée use his exotic setting and its local colour? In both Spain and Corsica he was dealing with exotic regions with an image in the mind of the public: in the case of Spain, an image to which he had himself made a significant contribution (in the *Théâtre de Clara Gazul*) as a land of passionate women and violence, of the Inquisition and lecherous monks. After his first visit to Spain (1830) his *Lettres d'Espagne*, with Hugo's ballads and Musset's *Contes d'Espagne et d'Italie*, helped reinforce the image of a Spain 'de *cachucha*, de castagnettes, de *majos*, de *manolas*, de moines, de contrebandiers et de combats de taureaux' (Gautier, *Voyage en Espagne*, p.269), of poor inns, bandits and superstition. By the late 1830s France was in the grip of the second wave of an enthusiasm for Spain, seen above all in boulevard plays and popular literature. Nor was Mérimée, in *Carmen*, individual in the aspects of Spain that he portrayed. Both Romantic writers (e.g. Hugo in *Notre-Dame de Paris*) and serious travellers (George Borrow) had evoked gypsy life as picturesque and mysterious. January 1839 saw the creation of the ballet *La Gypsy* at the Opéra and the *vaudeville La Gitana* at the Gymnase; 1843, *Les Contrebandiers de la Sierra Nevada*, at the Théâtre des Variétés; 1837 and 1838 saw plays on Don Pedro and Maria Padilla (see *Car.*, pp.133 and 163; Mérimée was working on his historical study *Histoire de don Pèdre* in 1843-47).

---

[9] *Voyage en Espagne* suivi de *España*, ed. Patrick Berthier (Paris: Gallimard, 1981). For a fuller idea of the amount written on Spain, see Margaret Rees, *French Authors on Spain 1800-1850: a checklist*, Research Bibliographies and Checklists, 18, London: Grant & Cutler, 1977.

     With an image as familiar as this, one strategy Mérimée adopts
is to treat aspects as a topos, a set and known idea or event on which
he plays his own individual variation. The Narrator's first encounter
with don José is situated in a series of variants on the traveller and
the bandit in Spain. The reading public is familiar with Spain as the
country of 'le brigand espagnol' (Gautier, *Voyage*, p.370). Travellers'
tales develop a second version: 'I heard about brigands constantly but
never saw one', used ironically by Gautier (*Voyage*, p.180; cf. also
Car., pp.397-98). The typical traveller ends up thinking there are
none, after taking farmers for bandits several times. The first chapter
of *Carmen* plays ironically with this topos. The Narrator, travelling
in quest of archaeological evidence, says initially: 'Je ne croyais plus
aux voleurs, à force d'en entendre parler et de n'en rencontrer
jamais'; then he *thinks* he has found one: he is both wrong (it is not,
as he fancies, the famous José-Maria), which produces ironic
deflation of his preconceptions by reality, *and* right (it is the feared
don José), thus offering the Romantic thrill of an encounter with
danger: enabling Mérimée characteristically both to mock the cliché
and to indulge it at the same time.
     Corsica likewise, by 1840, had a Romantic 'image', with its
key words (*maquis*, *mouflon*, *vendetta*), and national character: a
wild environment (*maquis*, rocks, forests) where a fierce but
hospitable population of *montagnards* and *bergers* practises strange
funeral rites, exercises private justice (*29*, p.56) and performs rituals
of vengeance (the confrontation with the father's blood-stained shirt
had already in 1828 been criticized by a writer sympathetic to
Corsica as an anachronistic cliché relied on by 'écrivains routiniers':
29, p.193). We expect, in any tale of Corsica, the lunch with the
bandit originally destined for the Church who outlines his career and
boasts of his exploits as a modern Robin Hood, as in Rosseeuw
Saint-Hilaire's *Le Déjeuner du bandit* (*Revue de Paris*, 1831: *29*,
pp.242-44); we expect to hear about malaria (*Col.*, p.402) and
Napoleon,[10] and the sixteenth-century military hero Sampiero who
killed his own wife for dealing with the Genoans. Sampiero had been

---

[10] The links with Napoleon would be all the more in the reader's mind in
1840 as this was the year of the return of his ashes to France.

part of the Corsican literary tradition since Mme de Bradi's *Vannina, ou l'héritière corse* of 1823 which first included a discussion of how his 'crime' should be judged; Rosseeuw Saint-Hilaire had retold his story in 1831; the parallel made by Orso with Othello (*Col.*, p.330) is also an essential part of the literary treatment of the theme (*29*, p.237). Mérimée clearly expects us to be familiar with these; the references to Sampiero (*Col.*, p.330) would be unintelligible if we did not know his story already. The mosaic (Mérimée himself uses the word: *10*, II, pp.462-63) of familiar elements of local colour is achieved with deftness, with a knowing wink at the reader, as when Lydia uses a reference to Napoleon's grotto to break off a conversation with Orso that is in danger of becoming too serious (*Col.*, p.363). Above all they are ingeniously integrated into the plot. The exotic Corsican elements are all turned into *one* story around *one* figure (Colomba), to be played out in *one* village situated in the mountainous heart of Corsica (the real Pietranera is situated in the north of the island, near Bastia). The conventional scene with the father's bloodstained shirt is presented as something set up, staged even, by cunning Colomba as a climax of her calculated tactics to sway Orso, which enables Mérimée to get away with its rather theatrical nature. The local colour is dramatized: Valéry's observation that Corsicans will not accept money (*29*, p.278) is twice worked into the economy of the story, in the first case, in the setting up of friendly relationships between the Nevils and Orso after initial misunderstandings (*Col.*, p.323), and again later, when Orso demonstrates how far he has lost his instinctive Corsican reflexes (*Col.*, p.393). Local colour is worked in to facilitate awkward transitions: it is by a series of coincidences[11] that the Narrator meets don José, then Carmen, then (when with her) don José again, but the reader's attention is focused on the vivid details of the meal at the inn (*Car.*, p.99), or Carmen's magic (*Car.*, p.112). As Mérimée remarked in his study on Pushkin: 'Tout gros mensonge a besoin d'un détail

---

[11] Mérimée argued from the fact that he experienced coincidence in real life that 'les romanciers n'ont pas tort de n'employer qu'un petit nombre de personnages qui se retrouvent' (*10*, VII, p.201). But there are obviously ways of making this more or less plausible.

bien circonstancié, moyennant quoi il passe' (22, p.126). The bedbugs and fleas of Spanish inns (a topos evoked by Gautier as a 'détail
fourmillant et picaresque...de la couleur locale', *Voyage*, pp.213-14),
made it seem natural that the Narrator should seek refuge by
sleeping outside; it is then that he finds his guide slipping away to
warn the police, and himself warns don José, thus establishing a debt
that saves his life at their next meeting, and justifies don José's
narration of his life later still: none of which would have happened
without the bedbugs, which we accepted as a touch of local colour.
There is less coincidence in the central plot of *Colomba*, but it still
plays a great role in linking and precipitating events. For instance,
the death of Pietri coincides with the visit of the *préfet* on his way to
lay a stone at Corte. This visit is prepared when Brandolaccio
explains to Orso why the Barricinis will be occupied and are not to
be feared that evening (*Col.*, p.393); it is echoed by Lydia (*Col.*,
p.408); by its third appearance (*Col.*, p.419), the stone-laying has
become something we accept as natural, and almost a running gag,
which disguises its arbitrariness. It is the visit of the *préfet* that
justifies the implausible presence of the Barricinis at the vigil (they
have taken him so that he can hear a *ballata*), and leads to a crucial
series of confrontations; the local colour (both genuine, and enjoyed
as a tourist spectacle by the *préfet*) helps to cover the contrivance.

It is perhaps above all this integration of precisely recorded,
under- rather than overstated, elements of local colour into the
ongoing dramatic events of the story and into our discovery of the
characters that confers naturalness and realism on elements that in
nearly all cases are part of the contemporary literary image and
borrowed from (or echoed in) other writers. Spain is the country of
guitars and castanets; but when don José plays, it is part of the
Narrator's discovery of his Basque origins (*Car.*, p.99); when
Carmen dances with fragments of a broken plate (*Car.*, pp.134-35),
it is a natural part of her first day with don José, a sign of her
reckless gaiety and spontaneous improvisation. The effect of realism
is intensified by the working in of precise details that shock by a
certain brutality and by puncturing a conventional sentimental view
of human nature and the facts of life and death. When le Dancaïre's

band encounters the forces of law, they do not just flee, but 'ce fut un sauve-qui-peut général'; Garcia cynically shoots the wounded Remendado in the face to prevent him being recognized, and is concerned above all with the cotton stockings (a characteristically specific detail that fits in with the picture of smuggling); the fleeing bandits are forced to shelter overnight in a thicket, exhausted and hungry (*Car.*, pp.145-46). This, we feel, is what a smuggler's life is *really* like. The description of the funeral cortège of the Barricini sons rapidly evokes a series of things seen and heard: the noisy procession, with the wild wails of the women, set against the father's isolation in silent suffering (a single adjective, 'le malheureux père', shows fleeting sympathy). Coldblooded physical notations — the position of the bodies, the earth on their heads, the colour of their lips — highlight the mayor's concern, as he holds their bodies to shield them from the bumps. This and his stumbling gait anticipate his later mental collapse; any sentiment is kept at bay by incongruous comic notations: the deputy mayor stupidly anxious about what the *préfet* will say, the gendarmes arriving too late as usual (*Col.*, p.445).

Mérimée is *using* local colour for specific purposes in his stories; we can see this most clearly when the local colour is bogus. *Carmen* evokes at length the women of Córdoba bathing in the Guadalquivir after the ringing of the angelus, which prepares the Narrator's first meeting with Carmen. No-one has ever suggested that this owes anything to any local custom of Córdoba.[12] Travelling to the island, the Corsican sailor applies to Lydia a colourful compliment (*Col.*, p.331) that Mérimée had taken from Sancho Panza in the pages of *Don Quixote* (Part I, Chapter 30), included therefore not because it was authentic, but because it sounded so. Mérimée's primary aim would not therefore seem to be to give an accurate and vivid picture of an exotic culture, to evoke Spanish life or write a study on gypsies' life (*5*, p.1561), or to depict 'la Corse elle-même'

---

[12] At best it may owe something to an incident when Mérimée claims to have watched surreptitiously a woman bathing in a tent covering holes in the dried-up river-bed in Madrid in 1830 (*Moniteur universel*, 5 June 1853; see *41*, p.55).

(*28*, p.481). The exotic serves above all as a setting for evocations of outlandish, alien passion and violence. Mérimée is exploring issues of love, death, fate, revenge (*12*, p.116); the exotic provides a means of stating these more extremely, more sharply.

Corsica was the country of the vendetta and private vengeance *par excellence*. The first years of the Restoration had seen practical attempts to suppress banditry and vendettas that had become rife on the island, and a series of pamphlets had created a public debate on the administration of justice in Corsica (*29*, pp.123-24). How should one judge the acts of violence and passion that are characteristic of alien worlds? The issue is explicitly raised in the discussion between Lydia and Orso on Sampiero's murder of his wife (*Col.*, p.330). Mérimée's answer seems to be threefold. First, different places and epochs have different moral codes, conventions and laws; so that what appears to us now as cruel, or criminal, was normal or excusable then. Orso expresses this 'relativist' attitude with respect to Sampiero (using a phrase frequently used by Mérimée): 'Son crime a pour excuse les mœurs sauvages du temps' (*Col.*, p.330). Secondly, underlying these apparently different values are constants of human nature: 'La masse de vices et de vertus a été la même à toutes les époques; aussi, je ne pense pas que nous valions beaucoup mieux que nos pères, bien que nous n'assassinions plus. L'assassinat était une forme de leurs passions; leurs passions sont encore les nôtres, mais elles ont d'autres formes' (*1*, IV, p.28); these constants *do* enable us to see (and so judge) behaviour and character, if we do so, not superficially, not from the point of our cultural codes, but with a sufficiently detached reason. This view is illustrated by the melon-seller in *Colomba* who *is* just like a mainland market-gardener (according to the constants of human nature as judged by reason), but who *looks* like a 'féroce coquin' (making a superficial external judgement in terms of *our* cultural codes, judging by the *formes* rather than by what underlies them) (*Col.*, p.335).

Thirdly, the role of local colour is thus often to jolt us out of our conventional attitudes and assumptions, to make us see that our set ideas of human behaviour or moral codes are not the only possible, or the only defensible, ones (see *12*, p.147), and be aware of the constraints and hypocrisies of modern civilization. In this it plays a moral and intellectual role. *Colomba* draws parallels between the vendettas of 'primitive' Corsica and the duels of 'civilized' France. Orso refers to the vendetta as 'le duel des pauvres' (*Col.*, p.332),[13] with its rules (the 'défi en règle'), to make us see that the vendetta is not different in essence, just a local variant, due to historical circumstance (the Genoan domination had led to the lack of a trusted judicial system in Corsica: compare Colomba's remark that one cannot rely on 'les robes noires', *Col.*, p.425), and in a sense less futile than the duel has become.[14] Orso attempts (not without manipulation) to turn vengeance into a duel (*Col.*, p.419), i.e. the sort of ritual violence that he considers legitimate (as does don José with Garcia: *Car.*, p.154): we are encouraged to see foreign 'savagery' as parallel to something civilized that we accept unthinkingly. But the role of local colour can also be to evoke (once we have overcome our limiting moral code) admiration for the individual energy that alien or primitive codes can sometimes develop and which is lacking in the civilized modern world. As with Lydia's admiration for the 'sauvage' and the 'énergique', this is an emotional and aesthetic reaction, rather than one of moral approval. As the Narrator observes of the statue of *La Vénus d'Ille*, 'l'énergie, même dans les mauvaises passions, excite toujours en nous un étonnement et une espèce d'admiration involontaire' (*Col.*, p.298). It is Mérimée's reaction to bullfights and to war: 'Il faut en convenir, à la honte de l'humanité, la guerre avec toutes ses horreurs a des charmes extraordinaires, surtout pour ceux qui la contemplent à l'abri' (*Car.*, p.358); to bandits: 'Je suis de ceux qui goûtent fort les bandits, non que j'aime à les rencontrer sur mon chemin; mais, malgré moi, l'énergie de ces hommes en lutte contre la société m'arrache une admiration dont j'ai honte' (*2*, IX, pp.10-11). Each

---

[13] Cf. *Lettres d'Espagne*: 'L'assassinat est ici le duel des pauvres gens' (*Car.*, p.381). The parallel is a standard one in writing on the vendetta in Corsica (see *29*, p.47); it is developed at length in Mérimée's *Notes d'un voyage en Corse*.

[14] See 'Branthôme', in *1*, IV: 'A la fin du xvie siècle on ne se battait pas comme aujourd'hui, pour prouver qu'on fait plus de cas de l'opinion que de la vie; on se battait pour se venger ou se défaire d'un ennemi' (p.84).

time he expresses a reservation, either about the moral implications
of the 'admiration', or the practical desirability of first-hand experience in real life of the energy that arouses it.[15]

In *Colomba* and *Carmen* this ambiguous response is embodied
in the heroines, in whom Mérimée's admiration for their energy,
lucidity, independence and pride is set against an awareness of their
ferocity and cruelty (see Chapter 4). Conversely, an awareness of the
advantages of the rule of the law, represented by the *préfet* in
Colomba, is coupled with a sense of his dull mediocrity: he is a
comic figure with his repeated exasperation with Corsica: 'Quel
pays!' (*Col.*, pp.418, 419); and in both stories, the law always arrives
too late (*Col.*, p.445; *Car.*, p.105). There is a sense of the ambiva-
lence of both the primitive and the civilized, and that what the artist
might find most exciting is not necessarily what is most comfortable
to live with.

Orso and the local code

It might be helpful to try to distinguish the moral question (how do
we judge an alien code?) from the complications introduced by
Mérimée's aesthetic admiration for the primitive. It is in *Colomba*
that the moral question is most clearly posed, but the sense of the
conflict of a primitive code (based on clan solidarity and private
vengeance) with the values of civilization is ultimately blurred.
Mérimée presents the vendetta between the della Rebbias and the
Barricinis (at the start of Chapter 6) as intrinsically absurd: it has no
determinable cause, and the feud is kept going like a sort of cold
war, given a political dimension by being linked to the nineteenth-
century conflict between Bonapartists (the della Rebbias) and
supporters of the Bourbons (the Barricinis), until it is reactivated by
Mme della Rebbia's funeral. In the present circumstances, however,
the feud turns into a scheme, leading to forgery and murder, whereby

---

[15] Cf. *10*, II, p.16, on the atrocities of the civil war in Spain: 'Les faiseurs de
roman doivent se réjouir qu'on leur laisse un pays poétique et sauvage, mais
il est bien triste de voir tant d'honnêtes gens sacrifiés ainsi pour les menus
plaisirs de quelques imbéciles.'

the mayor seeks to humiliate the della Rebbias by gaining possession of a stream and a mill. It rapidly becomes, not so much an ongoing feud between two clans (the essence of vendettas at the time, *32*, p.187), but a struggle between *real* villains (perfidious and underhand) and the heroic, noble, innocent della Rebbias; not so much a Corsican vendetta as a Western, where (as in a Western) the final shoot-out takes place between the representatives of the two sides, good and evil, because of the powerlessness of the law, subverted by a corrupt mayor. Barricini is characterized as avaricious, cheating, and cowardly; his sons are arrogant thugs. When Barricini makes his first appearance, it is difficult to look more of a villain (the physical betrays the moral): 'un vieillard voûté, au teint bilieux, cachant mal sous ses lunettes vertes un regard timide et inquiet' (*Col.*, p.399). Our sympathy is kept unambiguously with the della Rebbias. When Orso acts, therefore, we respond as much to a straightforward defender of justice as to someone maintaining a specifically Corsican code of honour.

The development of the story down to chapter 17 presents an Orso caught between two codes: the Corsican honour of his upbringing, based on family solidarity, in terms of which he should avenge his father's murder, but which he now judges primitive; and the civilized values he now holds to that result from his career on the continent, in terms of which he can seek satisfaction for private insult in a duel, but which rely on the law to punish crime. On his return to Corsica he feels a conflict set up between the two: 'Je me sens redevenir sauvage depuis que j'ai mis le pied dans cette île' (*Col.*, p.360). Colomba expects him to execute vengeance, he tells Lydia (*Col.*, p.361); Lydia throws her weight behind the values of civilization, and her gift of the ring makes explicit the idea of an inner conflict. In the body of the *nouvelle* Colomba sets up a series of incidents to exert indirect pressures on Orso (indirect because she knows he doesn't believe in the guilt of the Barricinis) which lead up to her explicit call to revenge, with the visit to the *mucchio*, and showing Orso the shirt and bullets. Set against this is a contrary attempt to defuse the call to vengeance: by Lydia, by his conscious thoughts, in which he dismisses Corsican attitudes as 'préjugés grossiers' (*Col.*, p.378), by the *préfet*. Alone in Pietranera, Orso 'voyait avec effroi cette attente où chacun semblait être de sa conduite à l'égard des Barricini' (*Col.*, p.378). This 'attente' is in part ours too: an expectation of a resolution of the conflict. The potentially tragic implications of the situation are that he would seem to have to choose to sacrifice either his acquired idea of civilization, and Lydia, or the Corsican values of his family and Colomba, and what he thinks that he owes to his father; and both are important and valuable to him. There is no real possibility of his forging and living his own *individual* code, like a hero of Stendhal, independently of the code of a group. The only compromise he can think of (a duel) is one no-one else, not even the *préfet*, can understand.

But if we and he expect a resolution 'dans ce combat entre sa conscience et ses préjugés' (*Col.*, p.386), it is avoided. As he rides to meet Lydia, Orso, though now convinced that the Barricinis are not innocent, is still caught between conflicting feelings, 'agité par des résolutions contraires' (*Col.*, p.432): his anger at the mutilation of his horse, his memory of his father, the threats of Barricinis, make him want a confrontation and a showdown; his promise to the *préfet*, his fear of missing Lydia restrain him. Mérimée is not so much indulging in psychological analysis, as elaborating the conflict to increase the mood of suspense and expectation. Then Mérimée shifts from Orso's thoughts to observation of the terrain as he sees it. His immediate response to spotting Orlanduccio is to 'se mettre en défense', and to their shots, to fire back. Mérimée describes, not his thoughts, but his actions, and they are the reflexes of a soldier (and his skill as a shot has been carefully prepared: *Col.*, p.343). To defend oneself in these circumstances is self-defence; it is not necessary (as Michaut observed: *31*, p.56) to have a murdered father, or to be a Corsican. The tragic potential has been sidestepped in a solution that keeps both Lydia and Colomba happy: Orso does not compromise his principles by defending himself, and he does avenge his father's murder. Michaut describes this avoidance of a real resolution of the conflict as a mystification, and one can indeed see many other occasions when Mérimée deliberately misleads the

reader: with pastiche translations that purport to be Spanish plays
(*Clara Gazul*) or Illyrian ballads (*La Guzla*), with refusals to explain
mysterious events (*La Vénus d'Ille*, *Lokis*), with deliberately
misleading presentation of events that are subsequently explained by
being seen from a different angle (*Djoûmane*: it was a dream). It is
certainly an evasion of what the reader had been led to expect,
namely that Orso would have to choose between the civilized and
the Corsican codes; the evasion was in fact pointed out by Sainte-
Beuve, reviewing *Colomba* in 1841. He argued that it would have
been bolder to make Orso yield directly to Colomba, 'le génie corse
en personne'; a really primitive narrator would have done so; 'mais,
pour nous, lecteurs modernes, qui, après tout, ne sommes pas Corses,
qui nous intéressons à Orso et qui tenons fort à ce qu'il ne finisse ni
par le maquis ni par les galères, nous sommes heureux de la dextérité
du romancier' in reconciling the logic of the action, which was
leading to confrontation, and the reader's desire that Orso be kept
both courageous and innocent in the eyes of the law (*33*, pp.488-89).
From this point of view the plot of *Colomba*, insofar as it is centred
on Orso, has been constructed to entertain (with tension and
suspense in the feud, coupled with a sentimental love-interest
lightened with comedy) rather than to challenge. Mérimée has
engineered a plot without any human loss (except for the totally
antipathetic Barricinis) and consequently without any real growth in
awareness on the part of Orso, any real discovery about himself as
the result of his actions.

But Mérimée's solution is arguably more than a piece of deft
sleight of hand; it does make a general moral point, albeit not one we
expected ('origins are more powerful than education', say, or alternatively 'reason and education can triumph over the primitive'). By
presenting the events of the ambush as Orso perceives them and
responds to them instinctively — he only has time to exclaim:
'Misérable lâche', as he realizes what is going on — Mérimée
suggests how little we can really prepare to make crucial choices,
how much depends on reflex, the chance of the moment, fate,
circumstances. Just as much as in *Tamango*, with its apparently
absurd reversals of fortune, men are 'pawns in an enormous practical

joke on mankind played by an ironical Providence' (*46*, p.133); and
after the ambush, like Tamango after the slaves' revolt, Orso,
wounded and taken off to the *maquis* by Brandolaccio, loses his grip
on the situation. This pessimistic sense of human powerlessness in
the face of a quirky fate, or chance, or instinct, is ideal material for
the *nouvelle* which can content itself with wryly noting it, without
explaining why: there *is* no explanation (as Paul Bourget put it, for
Mérimée, 'l'existence humaine n'a pas de sens humain', *20*, p.19). 'La
vie est un combat' was the message on Lydia's ring; but in Mérimée's
world it is foolish to think we can strive to control our passions (any
more than Szémioth can control his bear-like instincts in *Lokis*), or
plan with respect to the future, know either what fate will bring or
how we will behave. We do not know why Carmen throws the
flower at don José (*Car.*, p.147): the progression from soldier to
smuggler and murderer is not only rapid and easy, but one scarcely
notices it happening, as he succumbs to rebellion, instability, and
violence. Don José tries to find Carmen in Gibraltar by tracking
down contacts, and fails; then she spots him by chance (*Car.*,
pp.149-50). The limitations of the idea of self-control are shown in
lighter vein in Lydia, overcome (in Chapter 19) by Colomba,
circumstances, and her own feelings for Orso. Ultimately the
ambush is not so much a 'mystification' (Michaut) as a
demythification (*29*, p.365), a realistic view of man in general and
the limitations to his self-control and ability to plan forward,
superseding a schematic clash between civilization and Corsican
vengeance. If 'la vie est un combat', this is so only in another sense:
Orso's lack of resolution and his attempt to master himself and the
situation are resolved in a fight, an ambush.

　　For the reader in quest of entertainment, Mérimée's avoidance
of the tragic possibility of the vendetta had, as Sainte-Beuve implied,
advantages: we can enjoy the excitement of the vendetta, but we do
not lose sympathy with Orso as, in the end, it is not really a vendetta,
and his act is self-defence. The exotic has provided excitement from
the spectacle of violence and energy; if we are left feeling short-
changed in terms of moral challenge to our own code, we can find
this challenge by seeing Colomba rather than Orso as the central

figure, and by considering our ambivalent response to figures such as her and Carmen.

4. *Woman: Instinct, Magic and Myth*

In *Colomba* and *Carmen*, if characters (especially men) succumb to the moment, to circumstance, to reflexes (Orso), to tendencies they cannot control or even acknowledge (don José's tendency to violence), it is the female characters who embody the ambiguous strength that the primitive code can liberate, and in whom the qualities that Mérimée most admires can be found: energy and perseverance, clarity of purpose, independence and pride, in single-minded Colomba rather than divided Orso, in strong-willed Carmen rather than don José torn between duty and love. But this strength is itself ambiguous, and Mérimée's aesthetic admiration is (as we saw) offset by moral reservations.

Difference and magic

Colomba is initially appealing for her apparent directness and honesty (for instance in the way she treats her brother's hesitant interest in Lydia), in her instinctive sensitivity to poetry (*Col.*, p.345), in her own poetic talents (primitive poetry was the only one Mérimée fully appreciated for its vigour and imaginative use of language). She seeks to win back her brother to the Corsican values that she represents, and to establish her family's position; to do so, she has no hesitation in calculating, tricking and lying. Her plan to win back Orso is, as we have seen, based on a calculated progression. She plots, from Chapter 9, the marriage of Orso and Lydia, calculating what the family stands to gain in terms of money and position as a key consideration. She tricks and lies in her mutilation of Orso's horse, and then to get Lydia to the *maquis*; she lies to the *voltigeurs* (Lydia is 'une parente du préfet': *Col.*, p.462), as she did to the *préfet* and to Orso (*Col.*, p.411); she does so with apparent lack of scruple because of her total conviction that she is right. After the ambush, 'le sourire du mépris sur les lèvres' (*Col.*, p.446), she exultantly humiliates Barricini (for whom even Mérimée shows a fleeting sympathy: 'le malheureux père': *Col.*, p.445), returning with the bodies of his two sons. Even the locals are struck: 'Il y avait dans la voix et dans l'attitude de Colomba quelque chose d'imposant et de terrible; à sa vue, la foule recula épouvantée' (*Col.*, p.446). Mérimée underlines this element of vindictiveness in her triumph by indicating the extent to which she is controlling herself and her followers, and is not simply in the grip of her emotions. In the final chapter we think the vendetta over, and Colomba transformed: 'Je ne suis plus du tout une sauvagesse', she tells the Colonel, referring to her manners, clothes and knowledge (*Col.*, pp.473-74).[16] Then she surprises and shocks us in her ruthless and unforgiving triumph over the wreck Barricini has become. (Orso is absent in this chapter, as if he were only an instrument Colomba used in her vengeance.) Mérimée suggested in a letter to his Corsican friend E. Conti that he had toned down this aspect of Colomba's character, and had sacrificed his original ending to the reader unable to entertain the *difference* of another culture:

> Son père vengé, je voulais la montrer occupée d'assurer la fortune de son frère, et je lui faisais organiser une espèce de guet à pens [*sic*] pour obliger l'héritière anglaise à l'épouser. Peut-être était-ce plus vrai de la sorte. Une dame à qui je montrai cette fin me dit: jusqu'ici j'ai compris votre héroïne, maintenant je ne la comprends plus. L'alliance de sentiments si nobles avec des vues intéressées me semble impossible.
> (*10*, II, p.463)

But, as Raitt observes, this original end might have given a rather insipid conclusion (*17*, pp.190-91). Her calculating side is moreover clearly present in her earlier treatment of Orso and Lydia, albeit

---

[16]The transformation is not unprepared: she had told Orso (*Col.*, p.384) of her desire to learn.

muted by the humour in these chapters, and her unforgiving cruelty is starkly underlined in the final chapter (Mérimée said in the same letter that he had been led to 'outrer dans la scène de la fin la passion de la vendetta'). She provokes from Orso (the response is clearly meant to guide the reader's) 'une admiration mêlée de crainte' (*Col.*, p.425), and threatens the civilized code that distinguishes between humans and animals, between the human and the supernatural, between men and women: she is compared to 'une tigresse' (*Col.*, p.414); Orso says: 'tu es, je le crains, le diable en personne' (*Col.*, p.425), and 'la nature a eu tort de faire de toi une femme' (*Col.*, p.424).

Colomba seems, when first met, transparent: 'Dans son expression on lisait à la fois l'orgueil, l'inquiétude et la tristesse' (*Col.*, p.341; cf. pp.418, 446). But the transparency is deceptive. Focalization, or point of view (see *45*, p.203) is essentially a question of how far an author restricts the theoretically total information he has about his world and characters. With the narrator in *Colomba* who is not part of the fictional world of the story and characters,[17] Mérimée is free to present the thoughts and feelings of one or more of his characters if he so chooses (internal focalization), or indeed to place no restrictions on what he reveals at all (zero focalization); or to remain 'outside' them and merely observe actions and dialogue (external focalization). Whereas we see extensively the thoughts of Lydia and Orso, with Colomba the focalization is systematically external, apart from a few glimpses into her thoughts, when they are fairly obvious. Mérimée is prepared to give the reader hints, but at the same time preserves the ambiguity of his heroine: 'En voyant ses yeux étincelants, son teint animé, cette alternative de préoccupation et de sang-froid, il eût été difficile de dire si elle était plus touchée de la blessure de son frère qu'enchantée de la mort de ses ennemis' (*Col.*, pp.443-44). She remains to some extent closed to the outsider. She is sustained by a dual confidence: in the rightness of the Corsican code, in her intuitive knowledge of who killed her father.

For all the differences between the two 'primitive' characters, with their very different motivations (family vengeance as opposed

---

[17]Termed by Genette 'heterodiegetic'; see *45*, p.252, and Chapter 5 below.

to independence and love: Colomba has a purpose, Carmen lives for her whims and caprices in the present), Carmen shares certain of these traits. She too has a sense of total identity with her own code and concomitant ruthlessness in the pursuit of her goals (whereas don José is torn between being a gypsy and a Basque). She is cunning, persuasive, mendacious: don José comments: 'Elle mentait, monsieur, elle a toujours menti. Je ne sais pas si dans sa vie cette fille-là a jamais dit un mot de vérité' (*Car.*, p.126). If she tells the truth to don José before her death: 'Je pouvais bien encore te faire quelque mensonge; mais je ne veux pas m'en donner la peine' (*Car.*, p.164), it is as if lying *is* life for her. She too intuitively *knows* the truth: the fate of herself and don José, and like Colomba is right. Both are compared to animals: Carmen has the gypsy 'œil de loup' (*Car.*, p.111), is compared to a cat (pp.112, 121) and a filly (p.121). In both cases the effect they have on men's self-control and reason is often described by using the term *fou*. After Colomba has confronted Orso with his father's relics, his state is compared to 'la tête d'un fou' (*Col.*, p.386); at the end, as a result of Colomba's vengeance, Barricini really is unhinged: 'un peu timbré' (*Col.*, p.475). So too don José, from his first meeting with Carmen when he lets her persuade him she is Basque, and escape ('J'étais fou', *Car.*, p.126). In that she is seen exclusively through the eyes of another character (don José or the Narrator, in their respective narratives), the focalization remains necessarily external.

Mérimée's scepticism denied him any belief in God, but equally denied him any confident nineteenth-century alternative faith in Science or Progress. He had rather a sense of man's vulnerability and weakness, an awareness of the role of chance in the universe, or the irrational in man. His only positive interest in religion was for the poetry and intensity of simple local faiths and superstitions, and as something naïve but genuine that he could set against the hypocrisy and self-deception of nineteenth-century France (as in *Arsène Guillot* and *L'Abbé Aubain*) where religion was adopted for advancement or appearances.

The supernatural is frequently present in both stories (Carmen's fortune-telling and magic practices, her belief in fate;

Colomba is suspected of possessing the evil eye; both heroines are accused of being 'le diable': *Col.*, p.425; *Car.*, pp.141, 165, and Carmen agrees, *Car.*, pp.135, 146). This is not because Mérimée believes in it as a real force, but because it can serve as a metaphor for the lack of control man has over his fate, for the insight and destructive power of his women, and, generally, for the power, cruelty or unpredictability of things that cannot be controlled or explained by man's reason. In the ritual confrontation of Orso with the 'relics' of his father, they have a magical effect on him: he is 'comme pétrifié', and turns to the wall 'comme s'il eût voulu se dérober à la vue d'un spectre' (*Col.*, pp.385-86). The crowd recoils before Colomba as before one of the maleficent fairies of local superstition (*Col.*, p.446). The presence of supernatural explanations (as with the evil eye in the final chapter) is not strong enough for one to use the term *conte fantastique*, where the reader really does hesitate between the rational and supernatural explanations of events (as in *Vision de Charles XI* and *La Vénus d'Ille*), and senses the inadequacy or insufficiency of a purely rational explanation. In *La Vénus d'Ille*, where Mérimée's association of a jealous and destructive female principle with the supernatural achieves its most powerful form, we are left with the real possibility (though it is only one possibility) that the unearthed statue of Venus (whose ironic smile, disdainful, ironic and cruel (*Col.*, p.291), anticipates that of Colomba and Carmen) has come to life to cause the horrific events related. *Colomba* and *Carmen* are rather stories where the characters fleetingly think they see the supernatural breaking into the natural world, embodied in the energy and will of a woman. 'Lorsque la tête me tournera, elle me poussera dans l'abîme', says Orso (*Col.*, p.360). The link between Carmen and magic serves to reinforce the idea of love as an irrational and insuperable force.

Opacity and myth

Carmen is clearly a tale of passion. As such it is curious in that Mérimée does not trouble to explain fully *how* the love between don José and Carmen arises, though don José's narrative does provide clues from action and dialogue which the reader can pick up and let the imagination develop: don José's recurrent rebelliousness points to self-destructive attraction to law-breaking; his conscious horror at Carmen's provocative first appearance hints at an underlying attraction; this is constantly linked to a possessive jealousy provoked by seeing her with a real or imagined rival; Carmen clearly does not want to be spurned, and she admits her caprice for a 'joli garçon' (*Car.*, p.135). The love remains nevertheless *inadequately* explained, but clearly doomed to incomprehension and disaster: don José's possessiveness is incompatible with Carmen's desire to be free, to choose and discard at will, and her fear of any form of confinement. These traits are linked to their differing cultural backgrounds, which come across both in general terms (attachment to home/nomadic tendencies), in details (don José at the start of his narrative is seen making 'une chaîne', *Car.*, pp.120-21), and in particular attitudes, for instance their attitudes to money: don José treats the offer of money as insulting (*Car.*, p.137), saves the money Carmen smuggled in to him in prison and returns it, and appeals to Carmen to start a new life on the basis of their savings; whereas Carmen is as capricious with her lovers as she is reckless with plates and money, which for her is to be tricked out of the gullible *payllo* (*Car.*, p.151, the English officer), not saved (see the origin of the fight in the factory, *Car.*, p.123), but dissipated for enjoyment, as we see in her treatment of the money don José returns. Mérimée is reluctant to indulge in psychological analysis, even when the narrative is internally focalized.

The narrator of *Colomba* remarks, after Orso has been confronted with his father's relics: 'Je n'essaierai pas de rendre les sensations du malheureux jeune homme, aussi confuses que celles qui bouleversent la tête d'un fou' (*Col.*, p.386); likewise when he first meets the mayor (*Col.*, p.399). We have just a pointer to the conflict of feelings in Orso, and a refusal to analyse them in any systematic or complete way, and an arousal of curiosity as to what they will produce. In the case of don José, we have a narrator who not only does not fully understand Carmen and her desire for an autonomous existence (see e.g. his final comment on her, *Car.*, p.165) but who cannot admit key aspects of his own character (instability, violence), who presents his thoughts in visual terms and leaves us to pursue their implications (in gaol, *Car.*, p.128, or dreaming of life as a smuggler, p.142: 'Je me voyais déjà...'), or who at key moments gives no idea of his thoughts or feelings at all (*Car.*, p.161, waiting for Carmen after the bullfight). This is admirably suited to the *nouvelle*'s interest in effects rather than causes and appeal to the reader's imagination. With Carmen and Colomba, the external focalization sustains a sense of enigmatic opacity, distance, incomprehensibility. It weakens them when we read a reconstruction such as that of Steuber (*43*), who attempts to relate Carmen's life chronologically and reconstitute her thoughts, however plausible it may be. They remain a mystery for the other characters who circle around them. Walter Pater saw Mérimée's heroines as 'painfully distinct in outline... like solitary mountain forms on some hard, perfectly transparent day' (*24*, p.15): they are awesome because both clear (decisive in action, abrupt in their demands) *and* impenetrable. What are characteristic are those key moments when we see them occupied with something very specific, but from which the observer is excluded: when don José refuses to respond to her suggestions about the Narrator: 'Alors la bohémienne lui lança un regard de profond mépris; puis s'asseyant à la turque dans un coin de la chambre, elle choisit une orange, la pela et se mit à la manger' (*Car.*, p.114); in the magic with which she busies herself before her death (*Car.*, p.163); Colomba heard searching her father's papers (*Col.*, p.409), or seen mutilating Orso's horse (*Col.*, p.426).

The heroine's opacity is also related to her mythical status. Carmen has been described as being 'en même temps que Robinson ou don Juan, un des grands mythes de l'Occident' (*40*, p.9); an embodiment in a narrative form that can be immediately grasped of a general truth that is more elusive. For Mérimée himself, the myths of the past were a way of expressing 'des mystères au-dessus de l'intelligence humaine' and difficult to comprehend otherwise ('Des mythes primitifs', 1855, quoted *6*, I, p.36). Carmen, as a mythical figure, is both memorable and open to interpretation. The wide popularity of the figure of Carmen may be due largely to Bizet's opera, but the seeds for this are there already in Mérimée's tale. It offers not just an opaque central figure, but also a very clear pattern of oppositions which account for its general appeal and immediate intelligibility (they may owe a lot to cultural attitudes of the nineteenth century, as Maingueneau shows, but are still easy to grasp). The main oppositions are built on the contrast between don José and Carmen, associated respectively with the North (his Basque origins) and the mountains, and with the South, the warmth and sensuality of the 'oriental' gypsy race and Andalusía. On this opposition a whole series of contrasts can be elaborated. Don José is attached to his home, Carmen is a wandering gypsy, ready to invent a birthplace to suit the occasion (*Car.*, p.125); he is proud of his lineage and right to use the noble 'don'[18] whereas Carmen lacks a family name and tends to use of herself a popular diminutive, 'la Carmencita'. Duty and honour are contrasted with Carmen who combines what is forbidden, criminality and sexuality; Carmen's improvised castanets and dancing are set against the 'tambours qui battaient la retraite' (*Car.*, pp.134-35). The army is pre-eminently associated with constraint: with fixed ranks, orders given, uniforms (whose colour is mocked by Carmen when she calls him 'canari', a cage-bird), quarters, roll-call, a regulated time, a life of methodical repetition and collective constraint, set against multiple images of freedom which change from the relaxation of dress of the *cigarières* to the freedom of the gypsy life. Carmen transgresses boundaries: of marriage, by taking lovers though she has a *rom* and flaunting her affair with Lucas; of frontiers, by smuggling; of classes, by frequenting bandits, officers and Englishmen.

The first image of Carmen, emerging from the river at nightfall 'comme une force fraîche de la nature' (G. d'Houville, *1*, III, p.iii) establishes her as both associated with water, coolness and the slaking of thirst (and she goes with the Narrator to take ices at the *nevería*); but also with darkness and with treachery. Her irony,

---

[18] In the Middle Ages, all the inhabitants of the valley of Baztan were reputed to be noble (see *41*, p.142); this explains don José's obviously modest origins (his mother is just 'une bonne femme' (*Car.*, p.118), he is intimidated by the English officer's fine apartment).

mockery and wit give her a Satanic side; her disguises fool Garcia as
well as don José (*Car.*, p.147); in the tower of Babel of Gibraltar she
uses her mastery of languages to dupe the English officer. She may
use her 'magic' just to dupe the Narrator, but she encourages don
José to believe in her diabolical nature (*Car.*, p.146: "' Tu es le
diable, lui disais-je. — Oui, me répondait-elle'") and by the end
seems to believe it herself. The external focalization creates a
situation where the reader is conscious of her as a realistic character,
playing tricks, manipulating a gullible tourist in order to steal his
watch or a soldier who can help her escape, or who can be of service
to her smuggling friends; and at the same time the reader, just as
much as the Narrator and don José, sees her as elusive and
mysterious, wants to believe in her magic powers and the power of
love, and sees her as an embodiment of the destructive force of
passion, 'symbole de l'amour fatal auquel nul ne résiste' (*19*, p.221),
'a Venus of Ille in the flesh' (*12*, p.55), someone from whom the
helpless man can escape only by killing her, after which he turns
himself in to be executed. This mythic dimension is the clearer in
that the end of the tale seems inevitable and logical, even though
there are objections to it on a purely realistic reading of the plot: why
does not Carmen get someone to kill don José, as she threatened
earlier (*Car.*, p.157)? Why does she not escape, as he half wishes
(*Car.*, p.163)? This tendency towards a mythical reading of Carmen
can be seen in an extreme form in Dupouy, who presents her as
literally 'le diable en personne'; satanic because incapable of love,
and bent on the destruction of the male, don José. 'Si elle ne peut
l'empêcher d'aimer quand elle n'y trouve plus de plaisir, au moins
peut-elle faire que cet amour le conduise, de déchéance en
déchéance, jusqu'à cette potence qu'elle lui a promise' (*37*, pp.93-98).
This indicates how such readings tend inevitably to simplify the text:
it is a view that makes Carmen excessively preoccupied with don
José (to a greater extent than even don José's inevitably one-sided
account justifies); at the same time it is the sort of reading that the
text itself pushes us towards, since Carmen herself, seen externally
and a perpetual liar, remains elusive; don José tends to blame her for
his own weaknesses and failings; and the epigraph ('Every

woman...') encourages us to make a generalized value-judgement based on the character.

Once Carmen has been seen in this light, the possibilities of comparison are extensive: she has recently been compared, as a mythical figure embodying 'l'inquiétante séduction féminine, le charme pervers de la beauté fatale, l'ivresse inéluctable qui bouleverse les sens et met soudain la vie en danger', to Lilith, Kâli, Omphale, Circe, the siren,[19] not to mention the temptress Eve, Delilah, Judith, and Cleopatra (*37*, pp.16-17), all linked in various ways with magical powers, fatal attraction and destruction of the male. Of such figures it is clear that they achieve their mythical status and superhuman power not by what they achieve themselves, but because of the fear men have of them. The fear can be that of the man threatened by the woman in what he sees as his role: his prerogative of freedom of choice of lover, his position as dominant partner, as the conventional role of the sexes is reversed: it is Carmen who chooses don José, just as it is she who involves don José in her life of smuggling, who saves him after the killing of the lieutenant, who takes charge of the fortunes of a group of bandits, who suggests plans to kill Garcia and the Englishman. Tilby has presented Carmen as a castrating figure, wielding a knife (in the cigarette-factory) and depriving the inadequate male figures, don José and the Narrator, of precious possessions: causing don José to lose his stripes, the Narrator, his watch (*44*, pp.257-58). But the fear behind such destructive female figures can equally be the product of a male inability to control his own desires and actions, blamed on the woman whom he sees as having provoked them.

Psychology and patterning

Mérimée's refusal to explore the minds and feelings of his heroines also corresponds to his subordination of both the exploration of moral dilemmas and psychological analysis to other priorities: to tell a story, to give formal satisfaction. Even when he does pursue an

---

[19]*Carmen*, préface de Bernard Leblon (Arles: Actes Sud, 1986), pp.13-14.

analysis with one of the characters whose thoughts we do see, it lacks anything deep or surprising. In Lydia's internal monologue at the end of Chapter 8, her oscillations between attraction to Orso and reluctance to acknowledge it, between vanity at a piece of exotica that she could display and uncertainty about Orso, are artificially, or artfully, balanced. Nothing new is discovered, and the interest lies in our amusement at Mérimée's ironic elaboration and final comment: 'je n'entreprendrai pas de continuer son monologue, dans lequel elle se dit plus de cent fois que M. della Rebbia n'avait été, n'était et ne serait jamais rien pour elle' (*Col.*, p.368). Likewise Mérimée does not develop Orso's reactions after the ambush more than is necessary to point up a contrast between the celebration of the *coup double* by Brandolaccio and Orso's horror at what he has done. The 'meagre results' of character studies of Mérimée's figures have been commented on by Tiiby (*8*, p.16); one arrives at banal conclusions to the effect that passion leads don José to crime; that Carmen's love for liberty is stronger than her love for don José; that jealousy is a vicious circle, in that 'the more jealous José is of Carmen, the less she loves him and the more unfaithful she becomes' (*12*, p.52). Colomba's underlying motivation is never in doubt, and never develops: it is concern for her family. Her first task is to exact vengeance for her father's murder; thereafter her actions are dictated solely by concern for the future of her family (engagement or Orso and Lydia, then teaching Orso's son Corsican); it cannot really be said that she has any feelings of her own. 'Elle est Corse..., elle pense ce qu'ils pensent tous', says Orso (*Col.*, p.365). Rather than as material for individual or even ethnic psychological exploration, the characters are interesting for Mérimée as a writer as providing material for formal patterning.

What produces the effect of unity and concision, even in these longer *nouvelles*, is not simply a pruning to essentials, since Mérimée is ready to spend some time introducing his Narrator in *Carmen* and the Nevils in *Colomba* in a leisurely manner. The impression comes rather from the way the different elements of the story are held together either by recurrent motifs (parallel incidents, repeated events) or by repeated themes, to create the impression of a

limited area being explored intensively.[20] Both the Narrator and don
José meet Carmen and are seduced by her; on both she plays the
same trick with her mantilla (*Car.*, pp.108 and 121). The series of
variations she accomplishes on tricking, acting (at Gibraltar) and
bewitching is echoed, in the final chapter, by examples of the
gypsies duping tourists, showing baldly what was hinted at obliquely
in Chapter 2. The pattern of Carmen's fatal attraction is repeated
without any sense of progression in her, and all the men she meets
come to a bad end: the Narrator loses his watch, the lieutenant his
life, Garcia is killed, Lucas crushed, don José destroyed. So is the
pattern of helping someone to escape the law: the Narrator helps don
José in Chapter 1, don José helps Carmen in Chapter 3.

Overall the relationship between Carmen and don José
develops a broad thematic opposition between law and freedom.
There is both a contrast between the two in that they seem (as we
have seen) to embody these antithetical values; and at the same time
each of them is internally divided. Don José is proud of his Basque
traditions and nobility, but impulsive and unstable (he neglected his
studies for *la paume*, was forced to leave his village because of a
brawl, is constantly prompted to violence in thought or deed by
jealousy of Carmen); he constantly aspires to reintegration with
some form of order (joining the army, aspiring to promotion,
wishing a stable relationship with Carmen, wanting to start a new
life in America) and equally constantly is responsible for its failure.
Carmen may say to him: 'Ce que je veux, c'est être libre et faire ce
qui me plaît' (*Car.*, p.157; cf. *Car.*, p.164); equally important to her,
to her pride and sense of identity, are her gypsy allegiance and code
(she invokes 'la loi des Calés': *Car.*, p.134) and her fatalism. Her
attitude to gypsy law is in a way the cause of her death: while Garcia
is alive, don José has no rights over her because he is not her *rom*;
now that he is, 'tu as le droit de tuer ta romi' (*Car.*, p.164). In
refusing don José's pleas, she both affirms her freedom and accepts
'notre loi' and the power of Fate: 'Tu veux me tuer, je le vois bien,
dit-elle; c'est écrit, mais tu ne me feras pas céder' (*Car.*, p.164). For

---

[20]The technique has been seen as characteristic of the novella by Leibowitz
(*48*, p.16), but it is also found in many *contes*, notably Maupassant's.

the Narrator, too, there is a tension between his academic quest for Munda, and the temptations (bandits, women, magic) that lead him astray (see Chapter 5 below). What interests Mérimée is not so much the value of either these various forms of constraint (duty to friends and tribe, honour, family pride, academic integrity) or freedom (impulses of passion, violence, personal curiosities in the forbidden, rejection of control), as the tensions set up between the two. *Colomba* develops a related opposition between violence and the law (with reversal of our conventional expectations: the bandits are honourable and tell the truth, the lawyer schemes and lies), and elaborates variations on the idea of fighting and the different codes and rules that govern it. Mérimée sets in parallel duel and vendetta. Orso and Nevil, on opposite sides in a recent war, reminisce together about it: the fact that they had been shooting at each other at Waterloo increases their 'bonne intelligence', as had the shots exchanged between Orso's father and Nevil at Vittoria, whereas the families in Corsica have been nurturing a pointless feud for years. The theme of fighting is linked to three objects: the gun, the stiletto, and (with its motto) the ring; as we have seen, the motto refers both to the conflict inside Orso and the one with the Barricinis.

This interrelationship of motifs and themes produces at times very obvious symmetries: the history of the feud in Chapter 6 of *Colomba* keeps on coming back to obvious parallels between the two sides, with the two reversed versions of its origin, parallel insults (*Col.*, pp.349-50), etc. Brandolaccio is Orso's double, anticipating his fate with the murder of his father while he was in the army, his return to exact revenge and his flight to the *maquis*. Psychologically this may provide Orso with a constant reminder, and a reason (in addition to his weak state) to explain why he allows himself to fall into the same pattern after the ambush, without stopping to think; but above all it contributes to the formal *patterning* of the story. Doubles, as Bowman has noted (*12*, p.128), are frequent in Mérimée's fiction (don Juan and don Garcia in *Les Ames du Purgatoire*, José-Maria and don José); characteristically, the 'other', the double to the main character whom we glimpse in passing on the margin of the story, is often the 'real' one: the real Corsican bandit (whereas Orso has killed only in self-defence and can leave the *maquis*), the person who is really at the centre of mysterious events (Ottavio in *Il Viccolo*), the successful outlaw and lover (José-Maria in *Carmen*). Contrasting pairs can be set up to mislead: Orlanduccio seems the more aggressive of the Barricini brothers, but it is the low-profile Vincentello who is the real murderer.

Such patterning is often characteristic of short fiction; not only does brevity call attention to echoes, parallels and symmetries (such patterns are less evident in a longer novel), but it also constitutes a way of catching and holding the reader's attention. In this way the constraints of length bring short fiction closer to poetry, concentrating the attention on form, as opposed to content and message, on character as part of this patterning, or as something self-sufficient and often enigmatic, rather than as something to be developed at length, explored and understood.

5. Storytelling

Like any story-teller, Mérimée seeks to grip the reader by his tale (i.e. by the unfolding of events, not just by the intrinsic interest of characters or setting); as a writer of short fiction, he faces particular problems of ordering and structuring his material in a limited space; as Mérimée, a story-teller suspicious of the powers of fiction, he alerts the reader to the often misleading nature of narrative.

Curiosity, suspense, surprise

Mérimée presents us with vivid characters in extreme situations: a son returning to Corsica, island of the vendetta, after the death of his father; a bandit in prison awaiting execution. Using the curiosity of other characters (Lydia, the Narrator), he arouses ours: what will Orso do? who killed Ghilfuccio? who is the mysterious don José or José Navarro? how did he end up in prison, what was the nature of his relationship with la Carmencita? As we are in the world of the *nouvelle*, our curiosity is specific and limited rather than open-ended. Mérimée sets up as well a number of short-term mysteries to intrigue the reader (generally by restricting the focalization: we are told only what an ignorant observer, real or potential, would see). What is the 'énigme' (*Col.*, p.329) of the *ballata* and why will the sailor not sing it in front of Orso? What is Colomba up to as we see her cutting Orso's horse's ear? The Narrator's guide has left to summon the soldiers; 'après un instant de réflexion, je me décidai et rentrai dans la venta' (*Car.*, p.103): what has he decided to do?

In the case of *Colomba*, Mérimée exploits that way of sustaining curiosity that has been taken over by the detective novel: we are both following a sequence of events in the past (Orso's return to Corsica), where our curiosity is the basic one of 'What will happen next?' (will Orso yield to local pressures? will he escape punishment and marry Lydia?) and also trying to reconstruct previous events (the murder of Ghilfuccio), of which an incomplete version was given in Chapter 6. This gradual reconstruction is not always clear (how far do we lose track of the details of the case in Chapter 15, if not of the mayor's guilt?): Mérimée succeeds in exploiting the complexity of an ongoing feud, and the ambiguity of events (how is Agostini's silence to be interpreted?, *Col.*, p.357). Crucial revelations are carefully prepared (a mention of the mill in the first account of the disputed stream, *Col.*, p.353). The final questions are resolved only in the last chapter: who forged the notebook entry, and who exactly killed Colonel della Rebbià? All this is very deftly done, and only occasionally do we sense that Mérimée has strained coincidence (see p.29 above).

Knowing what will happen (or suspecting it) provides, rather than curiosity, suspense.[21] When Chilina warns Orso of Orlanduccio lying in wait for him (*Col.*, p.432), we too await the encounter. From the moment don José starts his confession, we suspect more or less how events will end: the Narrator has already witnessed his jealous anger directed at Carmen (*Car.*, pp.113-14); we suspect that she ('une personne qui vous a offensé', *Car.*, p.117) is dead; and we know he is under sentence of death for several murders. Moreover he consistently views the successive incidents of his past life in the light of his love for Carmen and his life of crime, and points to the critical nature of various scenes as he starts to narrate them. When he first meets Carmen, 'c'était un vendredi, et je ne l'oublierai jamais' (*Car.*, p.121); he is put on guard duty at the tobacco factory 'pour mon malheur' (*Car.*, p.120). His awareness of what his actions are to lead to contributes to a sense of fatality that he seeks to instil in his audience; so do Carmen's prophecies that to love her will lead to his death (*Car.*, pp.136, 140, 141, 156). Prophecies in fiction set up a situation of suspense, since we expect (from the conventions of fiction) that they will be fulfilled, but usually in an unpredictable way, thus reserving an element of surprise. In *Colomba* Mérimée

---

[21] For a development of the distinction, see François Truffaut, *Hitchcock* (London: Granada, 1978), pp.79-80.

uses this convention, both with the motto on the ring, and with the *ballata* (*Col.*, p.328), which is a prediction and also a call to action: the significance of the two bullet-holes *and* 'le cœur qui a pensé' is not clear until the final chapter. Such predictions give the characters' lives a *closed* shape and meaning, appropriate to the closed world of short fiction.

Subordination and relevance

For a writer of short fiction, even one ready to extend the *nouvelle* to the length of *Colomba*, story-telling is a process of subordination. In his evocation of settings, Mérimée is sparing, economical and relevant. *Colomba* underplays the variety and beauty of the scenery of Corsica. One of the few descriptions is of the 'magnifique panorama' of the bay of Ajaccio at the end of Chapter 3: it is slanted to convey negative associations of death and destruction, with its allusions to Vesuvius, to Attila the Hun, to family tombs, anticipating the moral atmosphere of the story, just as the isolated *venta* and deserted 'gorge solitaire' prepare us for Carmen's death. Other descriptions are integrated into the action: the 'maquis brûlé' and fields crossed before the ambush are seen from the military point of view of Orso, in terms of the cover they offer (*Col.*, p.433).

Descriptions of characters are equally selective and functional, and rely on a few small but revealing details. When first met, don José's movements with his gun and horse betray the smuggler as much as does his conversation (suspicion of the guide, knowledge about horses, evasiveness about his travels). The description of his appearance slides from the physical to moral and psychological traits: his tanned complexion 'qui *avait pu* être beau' (already suggesting change and loss), his 'regard sombre et fier'; there is no description of his costume until the Narrator mentally checks it against that of the poster describing José-Maria (*Car.*, p.98). The description of Carmen likewise only chooses a few details that count to create, not a clear picture, but an *impression* of a 'beauté étrange et sauvage' (*Car.*, p.111). All we are told of her costume, apart from the mantilla that she lets slip to attract the Narrator, is that she is 'simplement, peut-être pauvrement vêtue, tout en noir, comme la plupart des grisettes dans la soirée' (*Car.*, p.108). Generally Mérimée uses costume as a code, indicating race, class, or group: Colomba is 'la dame au mezzaro', contrasting with Lydia 'avec son costume parisien' (*Col.*, p.342). Equally revealing are Colomba's refusal to wear the Parisian clothes Orso has brought and her transformation in the final chapter (Mérimée does not say *what* she is wearing; her reference to her dress is sufficient), Orso's adoption of Corsican dress (*Col.*, p.383) and the mixture of costumes in which he goes to meet Lydia.

Names can also be useful codes. Their intrinsic meanings can be played on: Carmen, as a Spanish name, gives local colour, but also (in Latin) means both 'song' and 'magic charm'; Mérimée kept the first name of Colomba's Corsican model, Colomba Bartoli, but also exploited the sense of 'dove' in the variations on bird-imagery in the *ballatas*, and also the paradox of a name evoking peace given to someone so ruthless, just as her classical beauty (*Col.*, p.348) clashes with her cruelty. It is also worth studying what different characters call themselves, and how others revealingly refer to them, notably Orso (Ors' Anton' to Corsicans who expect him to behave as a Corsican), don José (Joseito to Carmen (*Car.*, p.135), José Navarro or even 'le Navarro' to those who see him as a bandit (*Car.*, pp.102, 103): he has lost his nobility and acquired a nickname like le Remendado).

In a narrative where Mérimée aims at simplicity, directness, and precision of notations, things play an important role as the focus of emotions and themes. The ring that Lydia gives Orso serves as a reminder against the 'mauvaise pensée corse' (*Col.*, p.362) and as a sign of her trust in him. It is also a means through which they can refer to their unexpressed love (Orso kisses it on leaving for Pietranera: *Col.*, p.367); he returns it because he is unworthy of her (*Col.*, p.449); in the *maquis*, she will not say anything that would commit her to Orso, but her gesture in giving it back does. The gun is linked to Orso's skill as a shot and his hunting with Nevil, to Colomba's pressure for vengeance, to the *coup double* and (because of its characteristic sound) both proves that Orso acted in self-defence[22] and plays a part in Lydia's lie on his behalf; it is given away at the end of the adventure. The dagger embodies the savagery of Corsica for Lydia, but she only wants it out of vanity, to show it off in London (*Col.*, p.366); all she can use it for is to cut the pages of a novel (*Col.*, p.408), a task to which it is not well suited. All are related in some way to (civilized or primitive) violence (the ring by its motto). They are not so much symbols, that is, concrete objects that are used by the writer to suggest an idea or theme, as would be the case if the dagger stood for Corsican revenge, but rather things loaded by the characters themselves with importance, and linked in multiple ways to the themes of the story and the feelings of the characters: in the case of the dagger, to Corsican vengeance, to Lydia's vanity, and to the contrast between Romantic fantasy and violence in reality. A similar role is played in *Carmen* by the Narrator's watch, don José's chain, the flower, the ring he gives Carmen and Garcia's knife, although, as they do not recur (except for the last), they play a less important role in pulling action and themes together.

One feature of Mérimée's technique that might seem to militate against economy is the reliance on dialogue. In *Colomba*, eighteen of the twenty-one chapters contain one-third dialogue (including the ambush), nine of these over half, and four over two-thirds. In *Carmen* all Chapter 3 is in theory 'spoken', and frequently reports dialogue, even on occasions when don José was not present, for instance the account of the fight in the factory (*Car.*, p.123). The high proportion of dialogue in the work of the story-teller concerned with actions has several functions. First, Mérimée is not just concerned to present action alone, but, with Orso, the pressures brought to bear on him and the choice he seems to face; with don José, the attempt to explain it (and in part, to justify himself) after the event. Secondly, he wishes to build up suspense, and talking about things in advance (vengeance in *Colomba*, the statue in *La Vénus d'Ille*) is one means of doing so. But above all the use of dialogue is crucial to the liveliness and easy flow of narrative. It

---

[22] In fact, given the nature of the wounds inflicted, the fact that there were only four shots would be enough to prove this (*31*, p.57).

serves to bring don José to life through his brief sentences, the simple structures of conversation (contrasted with the more long-winded archaeologist) and a smattering of local colour terms and proverbs; it distinguishes the *préfet* with his lengthy, banal and oblique address (*Col.*, pp.402-03) from Colomba with her abrupt and direct interruptions and outbursts (*Col.*, p.403-05). At the same time what Mérimée offers us is necessarily a stylized illusion of direct speech. On several occasions (e.g. with the *ballata*, or with the exclamations of the shepherd, *Col.*, p.427), the narrator makes it apparent that he is translating or 'filtering' the dialogue, and Mérimée is not averse to the distancing effects of narratorial intrusion created by this. A degree of stylization also preserves a uniform tone in the narrative, a literary elegance which at times seems surprising. Don José, a bandit (albeit one who has studied), can recall a moment of anger thus: 'Peu s'en fallut que je ne lui jetasse la pièce à la tête' (*Car.*, p.138); Orso can be as ironically literary as Mérimée when talking to his bandits: 'Lorsque j'avais l'avantage d'être votre commensal, je n'étais pas trop en état d'apprécier les charmes de votre position' (*Col.*, p.469).

Mérimée has situated *Colomba* in an island which is part of France but where the natives speak an Italian dialect; his characters are mainland French (the *préfet*), Corsican, and Anglo-Irish. Consequently up to four languages (not to mention a Latin-speaking bandit and an Egyptian inscription) are spoken by characters who may need translators to communicate with each other (Chilina's dialect account of the ambush is translated by Colomba into Italian, then by Lydia into English for her father's benefit: *Col.*, p.443), but who may use linguistic barriers for various reasons that range from preserving privacy (Lydia says goodbye to Orso in Italian: *Col.*, p.365), to the educational (the bandits in front of Chilina) and the amorous (Orso makes oblique advances to Lydia by quoting a love poem in dialect: *Col.*, p.322). This in a tale of deception, lying (by most characters), and forgery; one where decoding and 'translating' both gestures[23] and words is an essential part of coming to grips with

---

[23] Mérimée's use of gestures in *Colomba* repays study: from involuntary, revealing gestures (Colomba twisting her napkin, *Col.*, p.443), to coded

an alien culture, and one where misunderstandings are frequent
(*Col.*, pp.372, 375). The variety of tongues is related to the themes of
the story. In spite of what he claims, Orso has 'oublié le corse' (*Col.*,
p.425), as his offer of money to the bandits shows. He fails to inter-
pret correctly the mutilation of his horse (*Col.*, p.427). The *fermière*
tells Colomba to 'parler un peu corse' to old Barricini, and she does:
her final vengeance is achieved by talking. Carmen uses her mastery
of languages to manipulate others: she uses Romany to plot with don
José against the Narrator (*Car.*, p.112), Basque to appeal to don
José's nostalgia for home, and to dupe the English officer in the 'tour
de Babel' of Gibraltar (*Car.*, pp.149, 150-52); as in *Colomba* there
are four main languages (Basque, Spanish, with revealing local
accents, Romany, and a French Narrator), and both Basque and
Romany are used as signs of allegiance to a group, a culture and its
values. Carmen's gypsy proverbs embody her underlying attitudes
(the nomadism and opportunism of 'Chien qui chemine ne meurt pas
de famine', *Car.*, p.132), just as the set euphemisms of Corsica ('de la
viande de boucherie à bon marché', *Col.*, p.376) are revealing in their
attitude to human life.

Narrating

When we try to define the narrator, we are asking: who is telling the
story? The narrator of *Colomba* differs from that of *Carmen* in that
he does not play a role in the world where the events of the story
take place; if we call this (with G. Genette) the diegesis, he could be
termed heterodiegetic (as opposed to the homodiegetic Narrator of
Carmen, the pedantic archaeologist who meets a Carmen and a don
José whom he presents as of the same sort of reality as himself). This
does not prevent him from commenting intrusively and ironically
about local colour, moustaches, the English, and referring in a

---

signal (Orso and Matei's sign language as they board the dinghy, pp.320-21)
and universal language (Ghilfuccio's dying look, p.354); it too can be
ambiguous (Lydia watching Orso departing, p.367).

footnote to 'un ex-bandit de mes amis' (*Col.*, p.469).[24] Thus with the
two main possibilities of narratorial voice, Mérimée chooses
narrators who call attention to themselves. In neither case is the *je*
confessional: though it may draw on elements of Mérimée's
experience (the Narrator of *Carmen* owes a lot to his later archaeological interests, but is not the actual Mérimée who travelled in
Spain in 1830 and wrote: 'Les antiquités, surtout les antiquités
romaines, me touchent peu', *Car.*, p.415), it is essentially a narrative
device. This can have advantages in a short fiction. A narrative, with
a beginning, a line of events, and an end, is arbitrary, in that what it
is recording, insofar as it claims to be 'reality', is something
continuous and multistranded. To highlight or foreground the
narrator makes it clear that there is a distinction between the actual
events and his telling of them (between *histoire* and *récit*, to use the
terms of Genette); by doing so, it turns the arbitrariness of the start,
the story-line chosen, and the ending, to advantage: it is not
pretending (as a novel often will) that the account of events is
comprehensive, a 'slice of life', but rather it is *his* story. 'Je veux vous
raconter une petite histoire', says the Narrator of *Carmen* (*Car.*,
p.92). We accept, as readers/listeners, the events and characters as
figures in the narrator's story, one he has organized. In *Colomba* two
of the most obvious intrusions by the narrator are at articulations in
the narrative: at the start, and at the introduction of the flashback of
Chapter 6. This story becomes something self-contained (we are not
side-tracked into curiosity about the characters' life and antecedents
outside it), with meaning and a point (the worst thing you can say
after listening to a story is that you have not seen the point),[25] or
something with a shape ('That was neat'). Perhaps because the short
story often makes it clear that it is a story told, and highlights this
distinction between narrative and events, it has a tendency towards

---

[24] Consequently the habitual distinction first person/third person narration is
rather misleading: both sorts of narrator can use the first person.
[25] On this subject, see the interesting discussion by Ross Chambers, *Story
and Situation: narrative seduction and the power of fiction* (Manchester
University Press, 1984), pp.3-9.

either the provocative (a way of stressing the message, the point) or
the shapely, the formally intricate.

Mérimée leads his reader gradually into the story: it is more
important for him to guarantee the truth of events than to set events
into motion. He starts with familiar characters before moving
imperceptibly into an outlandish world or sometimes (*La Vénus
d'Ille*) seemingly impossible events. The Narrator of *Carmen* is at
first both trustworthy and, with his archaeologist's preoccupations
and priorities, faintly ridiculous; only gradually does don José
acquire the stature that prompts the Narrator to compare him with
Milton's Satan, arousing our curiosity about the cause and nature of
his fall and exile (*Car.*, p.100). The second chapter also starts on a
humorous note (at the expense of the voyeurism and gullibility of the
young Narrator) before the meeting with Carmen and don José's
dramatic entry. This isolates the central confession of don José,
different in tone, in tempo (urgent not leisurely), and almost of
texture — Charles Du Bos noted: 'Il se dresse au centre du récit
comme une sorte de menhir littéraire' (*14*, p.59), with its primitive
violence and passion. Likewise *Colomba* starts with a variant on the
familiar (for the nineteenth-century reader) and caricatural figures of
the British abroad, frequently portrayed as cranky men and colour-
less girls, and a scene of mistaken identity with comic overtones:
Nevil and Lydia think that Orso is a corporal and, patronizingly,
treat him accordingly (compare the Narrator persuading himself that
his bandit is José-Maria). Although the tone is lighter, both
introductions serve to introduce themes and oppositions that will
play a key role in the stories: the clash between different cultural
codes in *Colomba* and the strangeness of Corsica to outsiders; in
Carmen, the conflict between restraint and the forbidden; as well as
specific details that will be exploited later (e.g. nearly all the points
in Ellis's speech, *Col.*, p.317).

Mérimée combines two styles of closure. On the one hand
there is the predictable and formally neat ending that clearly marks
completion on several levels: symbolically (Orso's rifle is handed
on), on the level of plot and curiosity (Barricini confesses the
forgery, we learn who killed della Rebbia) and in terms of an

incident that echoes the start (food, sightseeing in Italy). Marriage has completed the Orso-Lydia romance: though this is not the end (presumably) of their love or their lives, we accept the conventional neatness of this. In *Carmen*, both Carmen and don José are dead, not to mention most of the minor characters; more importantly, the relationship between don José and Carmen has been taken to its logical conclusion. (In this respect we may have reservations about how far Mérimée has honestly resolved Orso's dilemma.) Thematically, in that the story has developed variations on the tension between freedom and constraint, violence and the law, the end represents a triple triumph of the law: Carmen has accepted gypsy law and Fate; don José surrenders after this final outburst of his violence; the Narrator is now merely a scholar. On the other hand, Mérimée often ends with a surprising twist — not the facile, mechanical surprise often associated with the short story, but a bizarre and slightly demoralizing turn: Tamango 'lands in the kind of slavery only an abolitionist British government could imagine' (*46*, p.131); Arsène Guillot's benefactress and ex-lover end up as lovers. Colomba confronts Barricini and repeats lines from her *ballata*, their sense now clear. Here we have a sudden sense of 'retrospective patterning'[26] in which the past is reviewed in the light of how things turned out; the surprise jolts us into perceiving something fundamental about the story and Colomba's destructive malevolence, all the more shocking in that the Orso-Lydia marriage had led us to expect reconciliation as the key-note to the end. The final disconcerting chapter of *Carmen* opens up a very different perspective on the life of gypsies, seen as curious specimens rather than fascinating individuals.

In the body of the story, assuming a high profile allows the narrator to take control of the pace of his narrative. A prominent narrator can jump over periods of time irrelevant to his story (the Narrator between meeting don José and meeting Carmen; don José explaining his escape: 'Pour le faire court, monsieur, Carmen me

---

[26] See the remarks of Barbara Herrnstein Smith, *Poetic Closure* (Chicago: University of Chicago Press, 1968), p.13; and also Marianna Torgovnick, *Closure in the Novel* (Princeton: University Press, 1981).

procura un habit bourgeois...': *Car.*, p.142).[27] Direct intervention and an appeal to the narratee (to whom the story is being told) is often the most economical way of explaining a situation or a character: 'On devine la contenance radieuse de Colomba, la honte de sa compagne, la surprise du préfet, la joie et l'étonnement du colonel' (*Col.*, p.464).

A homodiegetic narrator can choose to present events as experienced by his younger self, as protagonist or witness, at the time of the events he is relating (the Narrator travelling in Spain in 1830, don José meeting Carmen for the first time), or from the point of view of his older, narrating, self (don José in his cell, the Narrator in 1845). This alternative (which one could call the point of view of the hero or of the narrator: see *45*, p.214) is often crucial in Mérimée: the effect of both *Il Viccolo* and *Djoûmane* comes from their Narrators presenting events as they saw them *then* (one thinking he and not don Ottavio was at the centre of the mysterious events; the other, thinking the dream was reality), and concealing from the reader what they *now* know (he and don Ottavio are half-brothers and resemble each other; it was a dream). In the case of don José's tale, he relates the incidents of his past life after having turned to a life of crime and under sentence of death, aware of what his actions are going to lead to (e.g. his allusion to his impending execution: *Car.*, p.134), able now to see his fate as a whole. He contrasts what he knows now ('elle mentait') and what he thought then ('je la crus...'):

> Elle mentait, monsieur, elle a toujours menti. Je ne sais
> pas si dans sa vie cette fille-là a jamais dit un mot de
> vérité; mais quand elle parlait, je la croyais: c'était plus

---

[27] The presence of a narrator enables Mérimée to achieve this more satisfactorily than in his early dramatic works, where the transition from episode to episode is a series of 'jump cuts' from scene to scene. Godenne has noted that: 'Et, pour abréger,...' is from the fifteenth century a standard phrase for authors of *nouvelles* seeking to narrate rapidly or get into the story (*45*, p.21).

fort que moi. Elle estropiait le basque, et je la crus
Navarraise... (*Car.*, p.126)

Mérimée exploits the point of view of the older don José as an
element in his characterization. Constantly hinting at what is to
come, he creates a sense of inevitability and fatality; his recurrent
appeals to the Narrator call for sympathetic understanding of his
situation: 'Monsieur, quand cette fille-là riait, il n'y avait pas moyen
de parler raison' (*Car.*, p.151). The cumulative effect is also to
exculpate himself. He underplays the instability and element of
violence in his nature (skipping rapidly over the incident which led
to his flight from home: did he kill the other player?), shifting the
blame from himself to others ('He started the quarrel'), or to racial
characteristics:

> Quand nous jouons à la paume, nous autres Navarrais,
> nous oublions tout. Un jour que j'avais gagné, un gars de
> l'Alava me chercha querelle; nous prîmes nos *maquilas*,
> et j'eus encore l'avantage; mais cela m'obligea de quitter
> le pays. (*Car.*, p.119)

Don José's confession shows a refusal to face the truth about his own
lack of control (compare his account of the quarrel with the
lieutenant, where the killing is made to seem the officer's fault: *Car.*,
p.139). He tries to impose on the listening Narrator the idea of a
persistent allegiance to a certain ideal of honour (as soldier, as
Basque) through the vicissitudes of his past life (e.g. *Car.*, p.153,
rejecting Carmen's proposal to get Garcia killed in an ambush). His
narrative of his career shows the benefit of hindsight only in that all
events are coloured with inevitability; it is constructed as all narratives are, 'by someone in particular, on some occasion, for some
purpose':[28] to blame, not himself, but Carmen ('C'est toi qui m'as
perdu; c'est pour toi que je suis devenu un voleur et un meurtrier':
Car., p.164), overlooking the fact that when he meets her, he had

[28] Barbara Herrnstein Smith, 'Narrative Versions, Narrative Theories',
Critical Inquiry, 7 (1980-81), pp.213-36 (p.217).

already neglected his studies, been in a brawl, and perhaps killed a man.

The archaeologist seems to adopt the other available point of view by restricting himself to the outlook of his younger self. This is essential to effects of surprise, both in the first meeting with don José, and later in Córdoba: 'La porte s'ouvrit tout à coup avec violence, et un homme, enveloppé jusqu'aux yeux dans un manteau brun, entra dans la chambre'; it is only then that 'je...reconnus mon ami don José' (*Car.*, p.113). But the choice of focalization is not completely clear-cut. The Narrator's young self is naïve (we realize how Carmen is out to steal the watch that he displays so ostentatiously), inclined to vanity about his knowledge of Spain (*Car.*, pp.94-95), and fascinated by what is forbidden: by exotic sexuality (watching the women bathing, all too willing to let himself be picked up by Carmen), by magic, by bandits. In all three areas a gap can be sensed between the fascination that the Narrator felt then (in 1830) and the ironic attitude of his older self who stresses the difference: 'J'étais alors un tel mécréant, il y a de cela quinze ans' (*Car.*, p.110). The restriction to the point of view of the younger self is largely true only of information, to justify effects of surprise, but the moral perspective and self-awareness is that of the Narrator of 1845. The narrative maintains a delicate balance between the two. We share both the younger Narrator's anxiety, unable to follow the conversation between don José and Carmen, and uncertain of his fate, and the older Narrator's detached and somewhat condescending calm, expressed with a growing literary deliberation:

> Cependant la bohémienne continuait à lui parler dans sa langue. Elle s'animait par degrés...Il me sembla qu'elle le pressait vivement de faire quelque chose à quoi il montrait de l'hésitation. Ce que c'était, je croyais ne le comprendre que trop à la voir passer et repasser rapidement sa petite main sous son menton. J'étais tenté de croire qu'il s'agissait d'une gorge à couper, et j'avais quelques soupçons que cette gorge ne fût la mienne.
> (*Car.*, p.114)

Seen in this light, one role of the final chapter is to indicate a triumph of the older Narrator and the academic self over juvenile curiosities. The gypsies have now become just an object of curiosity, described methodically. His attitude towards sexuality is now the sardonic one of an experienced man (*Car.*, p.168); he now knows that gypsy 'spells' are just a way of duping and making money. The tension between the two sides of the Narrator, between academic duty and the seduction of the forbidden, seen in this exploitation of point of view, reinforces the thematic opposition in the story between order and freedom.

Story-telling in *Carmen* may thus be seen as a way of developing thematic possibilities: Garcia's view of Carmen would have been straightforward ('Il te l'aurait vendue pour une piastre', says le Dancaïre: *Car.*, p.155); there is more interest in seeing her from the point of view of a soldier representing law and order, even more when that soldier is a fugitive trying to attain social reintegration and whose narrative constantly appeals to cultural values (his Basque identity) that are a source of his incomprehension of her; more again when we see that soldier through the eyes of a restrained academic, but one who is also a Peeping Tom in quest of thrills abroad. There are many possible versions of Carmen — including her own (she invents her past for don José: *Car.*, p.125) and Garcia's. The point, for the writer of the *nouvelle*, is which will be the more interesting. (Compare the use of Brandolaccio's account of the two corpses, combining macabre jokes and a soldier's technical appreciation, to the horrified Orso.) None may be totally reliable. The start of *Carmen* alerts us to partisan narration, when the Narrator airily dismisses other points of view about the site of Munda. In don José's case his version is clearly also bound up with (self-) deception.

Colomba is full of variations on unreliable narrators and less than honest stories. From the moment we read of the conflicting accounts of the origins of the feud (*Col.*, p.349) to the *voltigeur's* account of the 'terrible combat livré contre les brigands' (*Col.*, p.464) that we have just witnessed as a comic skirmish, we are aware that no narrative is straightforward and natural, not even a neutral one (the 'judicial' account of Ghilfuccio's death, *Col.*, p.354); there always tends to be, to some degree, uncertainty about the subject,[29] or interest of the parties involved. Nor is the motive for this always self-serving (as when Barricini 'writes up' the events of della Rebbia's wife's funeral (*Col.*, p.352), or presents Orso's challenge to Orlanduccio as a 'lettre de menace', *Col.*, p.421). Immediately after the ambush, Brandolaccio begins to create Orso's legend by *talking* about it; crudely, jocularly, but also giving it a heroic dimension by the comparison with Sampiero (*Col.*, p.436). After the *coup double*, all, including Colomba and Lydia, see Orso as the *vengeur* of Corsican legend (and literary tradition); only the reader and Orso know that chance, circumstances, and his reflexes, have made him a hero.

Narrative can have a dangerous power: it can captivate, and Ellis's narratorial skill interests Lydia in Corsica (he himself has clearly been duped about the dagger he has been sold, 'garanti pour s'être enfoncé dans quatre corps humains', *Col.*, p.317). One recurrent ironic thread in *Colomba* is Lydia's desire to experience in Corsica the thrill of a certain sort of narrative, the novel, to see and judge all in terms of novels, to make of her experiences material for stories to impress others on her return (*Col.*, p.318). Her initial impression of Orso is that he is 'trop franc et trop gai pour un héros de roman' *(Col.*, p.324). When she hears of the murder of his father and the possibility that he might be returning for vengeance, he becomes 'un personnage' (*Col.*, pp.331-32), comparable to the historical (and literary) Fiesco. She makes him conform to one of the standard mythical figures of literature on Corsica (*29*, pp.364-65) — the fearless Corsican bent on vengeance — and begins to notice his handsomeness and manners (*Col.*, p.332). Her conviction disposes of any counter-evidence: his impassivity 'must' be dissimulation (*Col.*, p.333). The evident self-deception of Lydia and her naïvety keep her comic (in pursuit of the primitive, she sees Colomba as 'sauvage' for

---

[29] Not that there is, in *Colomba*, any ultimate uncertainty about events (as e.g. in *La Vénus d'Ille*): characters may remain in doubt, but the reader knows the truth by the end. Lydia may make up her memory of the shots, but we know what happened.

crossing herself before the meal (*Col.*, p.344), but fails to notice the primitive in reality, to see how she is urging Orso on to vengeance or to understand the boatman's allusion to the vendetta: *Col.*, pp.360-61). Both the 'fascination' of Orso and subsequently the idea of 'saving' him (*Col.*, p.335) come from her imagination, casting first him, then herself, in novelistic roles: later, lying in bed at Pietranera after the ambush, she paints a melodramatic picture of the imagined siege of the house, of wounded Orso, now equal to a 'héros de roman', and again puts herself at the centre of the story she is constructing, telling herself that he has been wounded going to meet or even defend her (*Col.*, p.447). She wanted to see bandits,[30] as Colomba points out (*Col.*, p.455); but when she does, she finds they are uncomfortably real. So through Lydia, Mérimée mocks the Romantic imagination that approaches reality in terms of literary stereotypes. But the paradox is that at the same time Mérimée is telling the story of Colomba's pursuit of a vendetta; so Mérimée can both offer the reader the excitement of Corsica, while at the same time pointing out the misleading or seductive powers of fiction-making and poking fun at the gullibility or naïvety of fiction-readers.

Thus Mérimée creates two sorts of pessimism in his story-telling. On the level of events and characters, the moral implications of what we see imply a sense of the limits of man's knowledge and ability to know himself and act responsibly (see Chapter 3). On the level of narrating, the story-telling by characters and by Mérimée himself often reflects on literature generally, as if Mérimée seeks at the same time to enjoy, to exploit and to undermine the fascination of the narrative power that the story-teller can exercise over his audience. Narration (and by implication literature) seems at best misleading, and frequently either unimportant and frivolous or nefarious (*12*, p.161): Lydia's dabbling in Orso's affairs is rather out of a desire for excitement and to see herself playing a role than actually to help him. Narratees are gullible: don José and the younger Narrator are captivated by a Carmen they want to believe in.

---

[30] Cf. Lauvergne, in 1832: 'Bientôt les voyageurs viendront en Corse, non seulement pour visiter la maison de l'empereur, mais avec l'espoir craintif d'y rencontrer des bandits' (quoted in *29*, p.255).

In his final proverb: 'En close bouche, n'entre point mouche' (*Car.*, p.174), the older Narrator, who seems to have lost all interest in his original characters, mocks the futility of all story-telling. Again perhaps the short story writer is, because of his sense that a story is something *told* to capture the audience, particularly involved in what has become a modern preoccupation: fiction's interest in its own devices, its awareness of its own deceptions and fictiveness.

Conclusion

A recurrent reaction to Mérimée is to appreciate his skill, and at the same time to use such an appreciation as a back-handed way of criticizing his work; Hytier saw something 'd'un peu mécanique dans sa perfection' (22, p.130); there is a similar response in Gide's criticism of the 'perfection inutile' of *La Partie de trictrac* (see *17*, p.133), as if the reader were exasperated at being unable to get *behind* the narrative, to find some depth or mystery. In the same way the approaches of recent Freudian critics[31] are outflanked by Mérimée's clear awareness of the irrational and unconscious forces in man (see notably the discussion in *Lokis*, *Car.*, pp.304-06) and the knowing and teasing way he plays with the symbols that they would invest with significance (rings in *La Vénus d'Ille*, keys and locks in *Il Viccolo*, snakes in *Lokis* and *Djoûmane*, the pot of honey in *Lokis*). They want to play with him, but cannot be too sure that he is not playing with them.

But the sense of play (and Mérimée treated literature as an amusement, knew that it was composed of tricks that could be manipulated) is perhaps precisely what is appropriate to the world of the short story, whose brevity calls the imagination of the reader into play, and which is most rewarding when we are confronted with something both limited (in events and characters) and susceptible of different permutations and emphases. Mérimée leads us not only to toy with different views of the protagonist, but different ideas of who that protagonist is. *Colomba* has been presented as the dilemma of Orso, observed as an educative experience for a young reader in that

---

[31] Notably Jean Bellemin-Noël, *Vers l'inconscient du texte* (Paris: P.U.F., 1979); Jacques Chabot, *L'Autre Moi* (Aix-en-Provence: Edisud, 1983).

reason and education triumph over inborn instincts;[32] or as an evasion of the conflict and a mystification (*31*); or as the drama of Colomba rather than Orso, a study of the primitive seen obliquely, ending with her triumph in the final chapter. In *Carmen*, the emphasis has shifted from Carmen herself, originally seen in the nineteenth century as the central interest (Pontmartin, Planche, *1*, III, pp.244, 262-63), to don José; Carmen herself has been seen as tempting and diabolical (*37*), or as the embodiment of passion and freedom, a feminist heroine reversing traditional ideas of woman (see *36*), or simply as a woman misrepresented by male discourse (*42*); don José has been read as truthful and sympathetic in his account of his tragic downfall, or gullible (*44*), deceiving himself as well as his narratee. One feature of Mérimée's fiction does seem to be to provoke extreme, categorical, and explicit judgements of his characters: Carmen as 'une vulgaire prostituée et une voleuse' (Siclier, quoted in *40*, p.11); 'don José me déplaît. Il est fort sot' (G. d'Houville, *1*, III, p.vii). The more attention the narrator calls to his presence, the less certain we become how to judge what he tells us (the Narrator of *La Vénus d'Ille* has been judged rational and reliable, but equally as falling into credulity towards the supernatural). Every such reading does precisely what Mérimée avoids: pinning down, explaining, judging. The more one examines the stories, the more one can trace patterns, connections, structures — see how they 'hang together' — and the more the central figures and events seem opaque and open to interpretation. The very brevity of the short story prompts the reader to invest details with significance in a way that he might not in a novel. 'Le nouvelliste ne nous donne que des constats. Pensez-en ce que vous voulez' (*20*, p.19). As the Narrator of *La Vénus d'Ille* said, confronted with the ambiguous inscription on the statue, 'c'est une terrible langue que le latin avec sa concision' (*Col.*, p.292); and as the word 'terrible' hints and the events of that story show, uncertainty can frequently provoke terror.

---

[32] Viktor Clos, 'Für die 10. Klasse: *Colomba*', *Die Neueren Sprachen*, 20 (1971), pp.9-19.

The tension between precision of detail and clarity of narration, and ambiguity of message and judgement, could be related to the persistent and unresolved tensions that run through Mérimée's fiction: between passion and formal control; between the primitive and the civilized; between distrust of and fascination with the violent energy of the exotic; between story-telling and mockery of its tricks and deceptions. Such a tension should always leave one with the feeling that one has not had the last word.

Select Bibliography

EDITIONS

There are numerous editions of collections of Mérimée's *nouvelles*; the following in particular are useful.

1. *Œuvres complètes*, publiées sous la direction de Pierre Trahard et Edouard Champion, Paris: Champion, 1927-33. Incomplete (12 volumes were published). Volume III (1927) contains *Carmen, Arsène Guillot, L'Abbé Aubain*, édition d'A. Dupouy, préface de Gérard d'Houville. Excellent preface and introduction, and contains contemporary reviews of *Carmen*.

2. *Œuvres*, préfaces d'Eugène Marsan, 10 vols, Paris: Divan, 1927-31.

3. *Nouvelles complètes*, édition établie, présentée et annotée par Pierre Josserand, 2 vols, Folio, Paris: Gallimard, 1973-74. (The pagination of Volume I was revised in the 1987 reprint.)

4. *Romans et nouvelles*, édition de M. Parturier, Classiques Garnier, Paris: Garnier, 1967.

5. *Théâtre de Clara Gazul, Romans et nouvelles*, édition de Jean Mallion et Pierre Salomon, Bibliothèque de la Pléiade, Paris: Gallimard, 1979.

6. *Nouvelles*, texte présenté et annoté par Michel Crouzet, 2 vols, Paris: Imprimerie Nationale, 1987.

7. *Colomba*, édition de P. Jourda, Textes littéraires français, Paris: Droz, 1947.

8. *Carmen, et autres nouvelles choisies*, edited by Michael J. Tilby, London: Harrap, 1981. Helpful and stimulating preface.

9. *Notes de voyage*, éditées par Pierre-Marie Auzias, Paris: Hachette, 1971. Contains the *Notes d'un voyage en Corse*.

10. *Correspondance générale*, établie et annotée par Maurice Parturier, 17 vols, Paris: Divan, 1942-47 (for Vols I-VI); Toulouse: Privat, 1953-64 (for Vols VII-XVII).

FULL-LENGTH STUDIES

11. Baschet, Robert, *Du Romantisme au second Empire: Mérimée, 1803-1870*, Paris: Nouvelles éditions latines, 1959.
12. Bowman, Frank Paul, *Mérimée: heroism, pessimism, and irony*, Berkeley and Los Angeles: University of California Press, 1961. A very rewarding discussion of Mérimée's fiction.
13. Dale, R.C., *The Poetics of Mérimée*, The Hague: Mouton, 1966. Attempts to reconstruct Mérimée's views from his correspondence and reviews; though these mostly post-date his creative writing, there are some insights.
14. Du Bos, Charles, *Notes sur Mérimée*, Paris: Messein, 1920. A series of often penetrating remarks, particularly on technique.
15. Filon, Augustin, *Mérimée*, 2nd edition, Paris: Hachette, 1922. An elegant and concise introduction by someone who knew the writer.
16. Hovenkamp, J.W., *Mérimée et la couleur locale*, Paris: Belles Lettres, 1928.
17. Raitt, A.W., *Mérimée*, London: Eyre and Spottiswoode, 1970. An excellent comprehensive study of Mérimée's life and works.
18. Trahard, Pierre, *Prosper Mérimée et l'art de la nouvelle*, Paris: P.U.F., 1923.
19. ——, *Prosper Mérimée de 1834 à 1853*, Paris: Champion, 1925. The central volume of a detailed three-part study of Mérimée's life and work by a critic who lacks full sympathy with either.

ESSAYS AND ARTICLES

20. Bourget, Paul, *Nouvelles pages de critique et de doctrine*, 2 vols, Paris: Plon, 1922 ('Mérimée nouvelliste', I, pp.3-25).
21. Gobert, D.L., 'Mérimée Revisited', *Symposium*, 26 (1972), 128-46. Ingenious perception of an underlying pattern in all Mérimée's fiction.
22. Hytier, Jean, *Les Romans de l'individu*, Paris: Les Arts et le Livre, 1928 ('Mérimée nouvelliste', pp.118-34).
23. Moreau, Pierre, 'Mérimée contre le "moi"', *Revue d'Histoire Littéraire de la France*, 71 (1971), 30-36. A concise description of Mérimée's 'vocation de conteur'.
24. Pater, Walter, *Miscellaneous Studies*, London: Macmillan, 1924 ('Prosper Mérimée', pp.11-37).
25. Sainte-Beuve, C.-A., *Portraits contemporains*, Paris: Calmann-Lévy, 1889, II, pp.196-99. An excellent early (1831) characterization of Mérimée.
26. Spoerri, Theophil, 'Mérimée and the Short Story', *Yale French Studies*, 4 (1949), 3-11.

ON 'COLOMBA'

27. Crecelius, Kathryn J., 'Narrative as Moral Action in Mérimée's *Colomba* ', *Nineteenth-century French Studies*, 14 (1986), 225-37.
28. Isay, Raymond, 'Une Nouvelle Interprétation de *Colomba*', *Revue des Deux Mondes* (1 December 1953), pp.480-91.
29. Jeoffroy-Faggianelli, Pierrette, *L'Image de la Corse dans la littérature romantique française: le mythe corse*, Paris: P.U.F., 1979.
30. Marcaggi, J.-B., 'Les Sources de *Colomba*', *Revue de Paris* (15 July 1928), pp.446-70. A cautious and sensible outline of the facts behind the feuds.
31. Michaut, G., 'La Mystification de *Colomba*', *Annales de l'Université de Paris* (Jan.-Feb. 1933), pp.33-58.
32. Roger, G., *Prosper Mérimée et la Corse*, Alger: Baconnier, 1945.
33. Sainte-Beuve, C.-A., *Portraits contemporains*, Paris: Calmann-Lévy, 1889 ('M. Mérimée', III, pp.470-92).

ON 'CARMEN'

34. Cellier, Léon, 'Le Mythe de Manon et les romantiques français', *L'Abbé Prévost*, Actes du Colloque de la Faculté des Lettres d'Aix-en-Provence, Aix-en-Provence: Ophrys, 1965, pp.255-68.
35. Cogman, P.W.M., 'The Narrators of Mérimée's *Carmen*', *Nottingham French Studies*, 27 (1988), 1-12.
36. Dubois, Claude-Gilberte', 'Métamorphoses de *Carmen*: un cas de réalisme mythologique', *Eidôlon*, 25 (October 1984), 9-62. On *Carmen* as myth; a shorter version, '*Carmen*: du reportage au mythe', appears in *Le Mythe et le mythique*, Colloque de Cerisy, Paris, Albin Michel, 1987, pp.155-63
37. Dupouy, Auguste, *'Carmen' de Mérimée*, Les Grands Evénements littéraires, Paris: Malfère,1930.
38. Fonyi, Antonia, '*Carmen*. Une histoire épisode de l'histoire: analyse narratologique et analyse sociologique de la nouvelle de Prosper Mérimée', *Récifs*, 6 (1984), 39-56. A sometimes forced but suggestive study.
39. Horrocks, Gillian, 'A Semiotic Study of *Carmen*', *Nottingham French Studies*, 25 (1986), 60-72.
40. Maingueneau, Dominique, *'Carmen': les racines d'un mythe*, Paris: Sorbier, 1985. Mainly concerned with Bizet's opera, but frequently illuminates the story too.
41. Pommier, Jean, 'Notes sur *Carmen*', *Bulletin de la Faculté des Lettres de Strasbourg*, 8 (1929-30), 14-19, 51-57, 140-145, 209-216. Many precise points, especially about genesis, that have found their way into

later editions, but are still worth consulting here for their crispness and coherence.

42. Segal, Naomi, *Echo and Narcissus: women in the French récit*, Manchester: Manchester University Press, 1988 ('*Manon Lescaut* and *Carmen*', pp.19-51). Male narrators blame women for their own crimes: stimulating insights from a different angle.

43. Steuber, Eugen, '*Carmen*: eine psychologisch-ästhetische Betrachtung der Novelle von Prosper Mérimée', *Zeitschrift für französische Sprache und Literatur*, 48 (1926), 273-304.

44. Tilby, M. J., 'Language and Sexuality in Mérimée's *Carmen*', *Forum for Modern Language Studies*, 15 (1979), 255-63.

ON THE HISTORY AND PROBLEMS OF SHORT FICTION

45. Genette, Gérard, *Figures III*, Paris: Seuil, 1972. Provides useful questions and tools for the analysis of narrative.

46. George, A.J., *Short Fiction in France*, New York: Syracuse University Press, 1964. Helpful in situating innovative writers in the vast production of the time.

47. Godenne, René, *La Nouvelle française*, Paris: P.U.F., 1974.

48. Leibowitz, Judith, *Narrative Purpose in the Novella*, The Hague: Mouton, 1974.

49. Reid, Ian, *The Short Story*, London: Methuen, 1977.

CRITICAL GUIDES TO FRENCH TEXTS

edited by

Roger Little, Wolfgang van Emden, David Williams